Hard Right:
The GOP's Drift Toward Extremism

Hard Right:
The GOP's Drift Toward Extremism

Mona Charen

Creators Publishing
Hermosa Beach, CA

HARD RIGHT: THE GOP'S DRIFT TOWARD EXTREMISM
Copyright © 2023 CREATORS PUBLISHING

All rights reserved. No part of this book may be reproduced or transmitted in any form or by any means, electronic or mechanical, including photocopying, recording or by any information storage and retrieval system, without permission in writing from the author.

Cover art by Rishikumar Thakur

CREATORS PUBLISHING
737 3rd St
Hermosa Beach, CA 90254
310-337-7003

Although the author and publisher have made every effort to ensure that the information in this book was correct at press time, the author and publisher do not assume and hereby disclaim any liability to any party for any loss, damage or disruption caused by errors or omissions, whether such errors or omissions result from negligence, accident or any other cause.

ISBN (print): 978-1-949673-94-4
ISBN (ebook): 978-1-949673-93-7

First Edition
Printed in the United States of America
1 3 5 7 9 10 8 6 4 2

A Note From the Publisher

Our goal is to make you think. We want you to react. We want you to respond.

Since 1987, the writers we represent and publish start discussions, arguments and even controversies. Love them or hate them, you can't ignore them.

Beginning with print and evolving into digital, Creators has been at the forefront of the media industry. We have been disrupting the status quo since our company was founded on the premise that creators should own their work, characters and ideas. Decades later, we continue to evolve as society pushes forward and technology changes.

At Creators, we support creators.

—Creators Publishing

Contents

Chapter One: The Descent of Decency — 1
What's a Party For? — 2
Contra "Too Late" — 5
For the Establishment — 8
Reaganism Is Dead — 11
Both Parties Digging Graves—Republicans Dig Deeper — 14
The War On Women Is Back — 17
A Little Too Much Reality in the Show? — 20
The Meaning of Ryan's Departure — 23
Being Decent — 26
Bully Wannabees — 29
Trump Smashes the Right's Ability to Police Itself — 32
LOL: Some Things Do Matter After All — 35
Why This Pro-Life Conservative Is Voting for Biden — 38
Trump's Republican Party — 41
Decency RIP — 44
What We Lost When the GOP Lost Itself — 47
Dr. Oz Quacks the Code of Republican Politics — 50
Cassidy Hutchinson Is a Heroine — 53
Mike Pence Sold His Soul for Nothing — 56
The GOP Can't Whatabout the Pelosi Attack — 59
It Couldn't Happen to a Nicer Guy — 62

Chapter Two: The Rise of Trumpism — 65
The Challenge for Republicans — 66
Patriotism, Not Nationalism — 69
Anger Games — 72
Contra Fox News, Trump Is the Threat to Civilization — 75
Don't Let Trump Discredit Patriotism — 78

Trump's First Victim—Truth	81
Trumpism Triumphant—Even in Defeat	84
Will Trump Face the Music, Finally?	87
How Mike Lee Ditched Constitutional Conservatism for Trump	90
J.D. Vance Joins the Jackals	93
Jonah Goldberg's Narcissism of Small Differences	96
The MAGA Perversion of Patriotism	100
Thank God Trump Isn't President Right Now	103
Liz Cheney's Star Turn	106
Try Trump at the Ballot Box, Not in Court	109

Chapter Three: Challenging Election Integrity	113
Thinking Impeachment	114
The 16 Things You Must Believe if the "Witch Hunt" Accusation Is True	117
Will Conservatives Give Russia a Pass?	120
Trump Thinks He's Above the Law	123
There Is No Return to Normalcy	126
Republicans Must Confess Complicity in the Big Lie	129
Sidney Powell Admits It Was All a Lie	132
The Real Steal Is Coming	135
Did the Jan. 6 Coup Fail?	138
The Trump Coup Is Ongoing	141
Are Democrats Up to Preventing the Next Coup Attempt?	144

Chapter Four: Getting Cozy With Autocrats	147
Where Does a Patriot Turn in 2016?	148
Why Would You Want Putin as a Friend?	151
Historic Snooker	154
Trump's Fatal Attraction	157
What's Missing from Trump's China Policy	160
US Blocks Examination of Crimes Against Humanity	163
Trump Always Had a Whiff of Fascism	166
Communist China's Family Values	169

What Orban's Apologists Reveal About Themselves	172
Putin Apologists Disgrace a Fine Heritage	175
China's Torment Is a Reminder of What We Have	178

Chapter Five: Embracing the Extreme   181

Ross Perot's Lessons for Today	182
Is the Party of Lincoln Now the Party of Lee?	185
It Wasn't All Steve Bannon	188
The Conspiracy Mindset	191
Who Is Really Burning Things Down?	194
Quazy for QAnon	197
Flight 93 Forever	200
McConnell Condemns QAnon, Except When He Doesn't	203
The Party of Violence	206
How to Disarm the Crazies	209
Republicans Are Rooting for Civil War	212
What Country Is the Wall Street Journal Living in?	215
Why Are You a Patriot?	218
The Right Needs Hunter Biden	221
The Normalization of Marjorie Taylor Greene	224

About the Author   227

Mona Charen

Chapter One: The Descent of Decency

What's a Party For?

Jan. 26, 2016

What is a political party? By the intensity of internecine conflict among Republicans, you might conclude that it's a church. Sen. Ted Cruz is among the leading voices of a faction that wants to treat the Republican Party as a confession—singing to the choir, denouncing heretics and damning sinners to hell.

This appears to be part conviction and part political calculation on Sen. Cruz's part. He's fully convinced that a Republican can win in 2016 by energizing the base. "The evangelical vote," a Cruz strategist told The Cook Political Report, "is the largest unfished pond of voters—it's a frickin' ocean." Convinced that dispirited white, evangelical voters stayed home in recent elections but can be roused by a sectarian candidate, Cruz barreled into Washington, D.C., in 2013 spitting fire not just at Democrats but at his own party, too. They were all part of the "Washington cartel," he thundered. Republican leaders were not just weak or ineffective—they were treacherous.

A terrible thing happened on the way to Cruz's plan to ride popular outrage with his own party to the Republican presidential nomination: Donald Trump offered an even more attractive brew of misdirected anger and indignation. If the Republican Party is now being hijacked by Trumpkins—and I truly pray that it is not—Sen. Ted Cruz is hardly in a position to protest. He helped stack the tinder for this auto de fe.

This is not to say that Republicans have enjoyed unblemished leadership during the Obama years—but that's not the point. Cruz indicted the Republican House and Senate leadership, and nearly all of his colleagues, for cowardice and cupidity. It was this, and not Cruz's firm conservatism, that alienated fellow senators.

It was all a carefully choreographed prelude to his bid for a great swell of white, evangelical Protestants he hopes to inspire to his standard.

So what is a political party for? The Democrats seem to have long since decided that their party is a coalition of interest groups: blacks, women, gays, Hispanics, Asians and unions. For the past few decades, the Republican Party has rejected identity politics in favor of smaller government and more individual liberty, more free enterprise, a strong national defense and traditional values. The party I joined did not seek to vindicate the interests of white people or the native born or Christian conservatives. It was open to all who shared its principles.

Trump represents a total collapse of Republicanism in favor of nativism, protectionism (that worked so well with Smoot-Hawley) and American-style Putinism. If he were nominated, he would be soundly defeated. Trump is viewed more unfavorably than any other candidate, including Hillary Clinton. He peddles identity politics for white people, but even most white people disdain that. For what it's worth, I could not vote for him, for these and many other reasons.

Cruz's strategy is a bit subtler, but also includes polarizing the nation—thus his dig at "New York values." As outlined by National Review's Eliana Johnson, Cruz's theory rests upon belief in the "missing evangelicals." Many pixels have been expended on the subject of voters who stayed home in 2012. When 42.5% of eligible voters refrain from voting, millions of African Americans, Hispanics and others are also on the list of nonvoters.

The case for a wave of previously unmotivated evangelicals flocking to the polls for Cruz is shaky at best. Consider that the last time a Republican won a presidential election (2004), evangelicals comprised 23% of the electorate and Bush won 78% of their votes. In 2012, they represented 26% of voters, and Romney won the same share, 78%, but still lost. Besides, the 2012 drop in voter turnout was much less pronounced in the battleground states that really decided the election than in places like Oklahoma, West Virginia and Arkansas, where an evangelical tide would not have changed the outcome.

Or consider the sobering possibility that evangelicals are not all that conservative. Among evangelical voters today, according to an NBC poll, fully 37% support Trump, with only 20% backing Cruz. As he watched Jerry Falwell Jr. endorse Donald Trump, Sen. Cruz saw his theory circle the drain.

The appeal to groups as groups is the bane of modern politics. The resort to shrill appeals to "base" voters on either side is shredding our national unity. To succeed, the Republican Party will have to win the votes of moderates as well as conservatives in states such as Florida, Virginia, New Hampshire, Ohio, Colorado and Nevada. A conservative can do that with a straightforward pitch to Americans as Americans. Anything less is unworthy—and unlikely to be successful.

Contra "Too Late"

March 4, 2016

Mitt Romney made a compelling and urgent case for why the Republican Party's soul is at stake in this election cycle. And speaking of Romney, his experience in 2012 illustrates why those who are shrugging that it is too late to stop Donald Trump are mistaken.

Attempting to stop Trump is not some underhand effort to steal a prize that he has already won. "Trump is winning fair and square, so why should the nomination be grabbed from him?" asked former Secretary of Education William Bennett. It's a fair question, but here's the answer: He hasn't won yet. Not even close. Only 15 of the Republican primaries or caucuses have been completed. Most years, things wrap up early, but that doesn't mean it's illegitimate to battle on. The 2008 competition between Hillary Clinton and Barack Obama didn't conclude until June.

Further, while Donald Trump has clearly won a plurality of votes so far, he has also failed to consolidate the party behind him. Yes, he has excited some voters to participate, but he has motivated many others to turn out for his competitors. Sixty-five% of Republican primary voters so far have chosen someone else. More importantly, huge percentages of non-Trump voters—74% in some Super Tuesday exit polls—said they would be dissatisfied if Trump were the party's nominee.

Trump's momentum has clearly been slowed since Ted Cruz and Marco Rubio teamed up to undermine him at the last debate. In the critical swing state of Virginia, for example, two February polls had shown Trump with 40% support. In the event, he got 34.7 and would have lost to Marco Rubio if John Kasich had not played spoiler. Pre-primary polls in Oklahoma and Alaska had shown Trump leading, but he lost both to Ted Cruz.

In the Nevada caucuses and every Super Tuesday state except Massachusetts, late deciders broke heavily against Trump.

Those who say it's hopeless to launch ads against Trump at this stage of the process overestimate how much voters know about his history. A recent poll found that 55% of adults had never heard about Trump University, Trump Mortgage and other disqualifying aspects of the con man's past.

Because the media have prostrated themselves before Donald Trump—offering him millions of dollars of free airtime—the only way to go over the media's heads is with paid advertisements.

Too late? Hardly. It's still two weeks until the critical winner-take-all primaries in Ohio, Florida, Illinois, Missouri and North Carolina. Consider what happened between Newt Gingrich and Mitt Romney in 2012.

Following his huge victory in South Carolina, Gingrich was polling at 41% in Florida in late January. Romney trailed at 28%. In just over a week—a week that featured a sustained and ferocious air war against Gingrich—Romney was able to overtake and defeat him. On Jan. 31, Romney got 46.4% to Gingrich's 31.9.

Trump's vulnerabilities are too numerous to itemize in this space, but the two main themes that beg for attention would seem to be 1) undermining his reputation as someone who "tells it like it is," and 2) casting doubt on his temperamental suitability to gain control of the world's largest nuclear arsenal.

The rise of Trump is often attributed to the corruption or failure of the institutional Republican Party. On the contrary, the response to Trump will test whether the Republican Party is beyond saving.

Trump undermines nearly every good thing that the Republican brand stood for. If he is the nominee, the party will cease to represent respect for the rule of law (he openly threatens to undermine the First Amendment in order to punish press critics); free markets (he promises high tariffs and a trade war);

fiscal responsibility (he opposes entitlement reform); protecting the unborn; opposing tyranny (see Putin, etc.); and human decency.

A Trump presidency is unlikely, since the press, which is coddling him now, will unload the full "oppo" file after the nomination, along with millions of ads from Hillary Clinton. But the key question for primary voters is: Will they permit the Republican Party to become the Trump party—i.e., trafficking in lies and threats, stoking ethnic and international tensions, endorsing Code Pink conspiracy theories, flirting with another Great Depression and degrading public life by the example of a degenerate?

It's not too late to stop it—but nearly.

For the Establishment

March 11, 2016

"Burn it down." That's the slogan of faux conservatives who now rejoice that the Republican Party is being smashed by a slick, howlingly transparent grifter. The urge to destroy has a kind of pornographic appeal to a certain personality—but it's a shock to find it so widespread.

The Republican Party is choosing an odd time to commit suicide. Obama's two victories were painful setbacks, but in the Obama era the Democrats lost 13 U.S. Senate seats, 69 House seats, 913 legislative seats, 11 governorships and 30 legislative chambers. All that stood between Republicans and real reform at the federal level was the White House—and the Democrats were sleepwalking toward nominating the least popular major player in American politics.

Republicans have managed to find someone who is even less acceptable. One-third to 40% of Republican primary participants are embracing a figure who not only will certainly lose the general election but also introduces an element of fascism to American politics, and thus demoralizes the Republican majority while delegitimizing the party in the eyes of others. It is Trump's unique contribution to wed authoritarianism—threatening the First Amendment, promising war crimes, admiring dictators, encouraging mob violence, fomenting racial and ethnic strife—with Sandersesque leftism on entitlements, abortion and 9/11-truther foreign policy.

And what sin has brought down this despoiler upon the Republican Party? Why are so many self-styled conservatives complacent about his success? Was it the failure to stop Obamacare? Please. That was never possible with Obama in office. It would have been possible, in fact it was probable, that it would have been replaced if Republicans held majorities in Congress and got an agreeable executive. But now? No. Failure to get control of the border? Illegal immigration from Mexico has slowed to a trickle and, in fact, more Mexicans are now leaving than coming. Failure to defund the Export-Import Bank? Yes, crony capitalism is disgraceful, but the irony of those who are offended by such things sidling up to Trump—who boasts of buying influence—is rich.

As Edmund Burke observed about the extremists of his day: "He that sets his house on fire because his fingers are frostbitten can never be a fit instructor in the method of providing our habitations with a cheerful and salutary warmth."

Here are a few words of praise for the Republicans. The Republican Party has become more reform-minded and more conservative over the past 30 years. The Arlen Specters and Bob Packwoods are pretty much gone. In their places are dynamic, smart, articulate leaders such as Tom Cotton, Ben Sasse, Cory Gardner, Bobby Jindal, Scott Walker, Paul Ryan, Tim Scott, Nikki Haley, Ted Cruz, Susana Martinez and Marco Rubio. The party has become more conservative and more ethnically diverse.

Between 2008 and 2014, when Republicans were the minority in the Senate, they blocked cap and trade, the "public option" in Obamacare and card check. Republicans declined to give President Obama universal pre-K, the "Paycheck Fairness Act," expanded unemployment benefits, a higher federal minimum wage, varieties of gun control, mandatory paid sick leave, a tax on multinational corporations, higher taxes on individuals and more. They passed bills authorizing the Keystone pipeline (which was vetoed) and trade promotion authority (the one issue Obama is not wrong about). They endorsed entitlement reform.

The American system is slow and balky by design. It requires maturity and patience to achieve your political goals. Democrats have been remarkably strategic, returning again and again to cherished objectives, whereas Republicans have told themselves that leadership treachery rather than Madisonian architecture accounts for their frustration.

Those who encouraged the "burn it down" mania and who popularized the narrative that a malign Republican "establishment" was responsible for the state of the nation may be many things but they are not conservative. Conservatives respect institutions and traditions. They understand that process is ultimately more important than policy outcomes because it guarantees legitimacy and political stability. Laws can be repealed. That is why Obama's worst offenses were not Dodd-Frank, the stimulus bill, or Obamacare, as bad as those were. His worst offenses were against constitutional constraints. He governed by executive fiat and got away with it, thus undermining the rule of law.

A plurality of Republicans seems to have accepted and adopted contempt for the Constitution. They will reap the whirlwind and look back longingly at the Republican "establishment."

Reaganism Is Dead

April 29, 2016

A longtime Republican conservative emailed me after Donald Trump's Tuesday night romp through the "Acela corridor." "Is the GOP now the anti-trade, anti-immigrant party?"

I don't think so, but take no comfort in the reason: Republicans haven't signed on to protectionism and nativism (or at least, only a minority has), but they seem to have lost all philosophical coherence.

The lesson of the Ted Cruz campaign is that the party faithful are not nearly as conservative as some had thought. Even among "very conservative" voters in New York, Cruz carried only 27%. Were Empire State voters still smarting from Cruz's "New York values" snipe? Maybe, but Cruz won only 29% of "very conservatives" in Alabama, 31% in Virginia and 41% in Pennsylvania. Cruz has worked assiduously to showcase his conservative bona fides, and while purists might raise an eyebrow at some of his foreign policy stands and his flip-flopping on trade, he passes every other conservative litmus test with deep dye. Yet even among very conservative voters, he failed to close the deal.

A lot of ink has been spilled analyzing why Trump was able to run away with Cruz's "evangelical" voters, but less to the vertigo-inducing reality that people who call themselves conservative, even "very" conservative, can vote for someone like Trump—a liberal-leaning, Planned Parenthood-defending, Code Pink-echoing, flamboyantly ignorant swindler.

Anger about immigration isn't it. I've always been a mushy moderate on immigration. At least with regard to Mexico, it's a problem on the way to solving itself. The "wall" would be the greatest waste of money since the feds created the Department of

Education—and threatening to dun Mexico for the cost is sheer flimflammery. Still, I was willing to entertain the idea that voters were really exercised about it as an explanation for the Trump rise—until I looked at exit polls.

Since Iowa, voters have been asked to rank issues by importance. In New Hampshire, only 15% of voters put immigration at the top of their list of concerns. Fifty-six percent favored a path to legalization for illegals living and working here. In South Carolina, even fewer (10%) ranked immigration first among issues of concern, and 53% favored that path to legalization. These results were replicated in nearly every state that has held a primary so far. Among Republicans in Pennsylvania, for example, fewer than 40% favored deportation of illegal immigrants, yet Trump won nearly 57% of the vote.

The exception to this rule is the large number of voters who approve of Trump's proposal to temporarily ban Muslims from the U.S.—a very new wrinkle on the old immigration issue.

Trade has loomed large in a few states, such as Michigan and Pennsylvania, but has been more mixed elsewhere, with voters divided on whether it helps or hurts the economy.

So the answer to my friend is that Republicans are not voting on issues; they are voting on personality and attitude, and thus revealing themselves to have fallen for one of the worst errors of the left: the progressive belief that all will be well provided the "right" people, the "best" people, if you will, are running the government.

"This is the end of Reaganism," former Sen. Tom Coburn, a conservative hero, told me. The three-legged stool of strong defense, small government and conservatism on social issues has been smashed. Republicans, or at least a plurality of Republican primary voters, no longer distrust government per se; they simply distrust *this* government. They dislike Obama and the Republican leadership. But they're ready to believe that an outsider will be able to bring his annealing touch to the economy, to the culture and to national greatness. If a Republican politician today were to tell the joke about "I'm from the government and I'm here to help you"—a reliable punch line in the Reagan repertoire—he or she would be greeted by incomprehension. This is a signal victory for the left: the triumph of faith in the state. Trumpites are reprising Barack Obama's "Yes We Can" with a new lead.

Republican politicians cannot rely on the healthy skepticism about government that was once woven into the fabric of the party. People used to know that bigger government enables more corruption; that the mediating institutions of society, such as family, church and community organizations, are better at nearly every task than bureaucracies; and that government undermines these institutions when it expands too much.

"All kings is mostly rapscallions, as fur as I can make out," explained Huck Finn, a good American constitutionalist. It's a lesson the Republican Party will have to relearn when this season passes.

Both Parties Digging Graves—Republicans Dig Deeper

Aug. 5, 2016

About 14 months ago, American politics began to resemble a B-level Washington, D.C. novel. A former secretary of state was revealed to have endangered U.S. secrets and possibly sold aspects of U.S. foreign policy to the highest bidder. Will she face indictment? No. But the FBI director acknowledges that the only way she could possibly get around security clearance is through her election as commander in chief.

The writer might have come up with a more compelling character. Hillary Clinton is robotic, shamelessly money-grubbing, calculating, secretive and promiscuously deceitful—to the degree that if she has any discernible principles at all, they're the wrong ones. When she raises her voice, which is often, it sounds like screeching tires. She represents the status quo in a year of change.

As deep as the hole that Democrats have dug is, the Republicans have bested them with a full-on suicide that not even a novelist would have imagined. A mob of self-styled "conservative" activists, jumped-up talk radio and TV hosts and Republican Party apparatchiks (oh, does that word have new relevance), and a plurality of primary voters and spineless elected officials across the fruited plain have signed on with a repellent demagogue who will destroy the party at its moment of maximum opportunity.

Now that it's too late, the rats are asking to be rescued from the sinking ship they helped launch. Former House Speaker Newt Gingrich hailed Trump's convention speech a "revolutionary moment" and reinforced Trump's reckless suggestion that NATO might not come to the aid of countries like Estonia in the event of a Russian invasion—among countless other lickspittle bits of analysis. But since Trump's terrible post-convention week Gingrich has discovered that candidate Trump is "unacceptable." He and other lackeys like former New York City Mayor Rudy Giuliani and Republican National Committee Chairman Reince Priebus are reportedly planning an intervention to get Trump to stop being Trump. Ha. Why now? Trump's ignorance, malevolence and instability have been on spectacular display for more than a year. Yet, men and women of honor and sanity boarded his cliff-destined train and buckled up.

There is no doubt that Trump has been his Trumpiest lately. He committed outrages against decency, truth and even his own best political interests at about twice his normal rate. In addition to dishonoring and insulting a Gold Star family and keeping up the feud for days (when he might have been discussing our dismal economic numbers), he vocally fantasized about punching out speakers at the Democratic National Convention; lied about his relationship with Russian President Vladimir Putin (though video footage shows otherwise); threatened to fund challengers of Sen. Ted Cruz and Gov. John Kasich to punish their disloyalty; claimed that he had received a letter from the National Football League complaining about the presidential debate schedule (the NFL denies this); assured an interviewer that "(Putin's) not going into Ukraine, OK" only to issue a corrective tweet later, when he "learned" (remembered) that Putin is already in Crimea; and claimed that he turned down a meeting with the Koch brothers—false.

Now, Trump has batted eyelashes at House Speaker Paul Ryan's primary opponent and mused that he would not support Ryan or Sens. Kelly Ayotte and John McCain. There's your party leader, Republicans. Well done.

In the Claremont Review of Books, Martha Bayles reminds us of the adage of two barrels, one containing sewage and the other wine: "Add a cup of wine to the sewage, and it is still sewage. But add a cup of sewage to the wine, and it is no longer wine but sewage."

Trump is a pathogen, a man who heedlessly promotes conspiracy theories (vaccines cause autism, Obama was born in Kenya, Bush lied us into war in Iraq, Rafael Cruz was caught up in the JFK assassination). He is either not fully sane or at least indifferent to the demoralizing effect that such lies have on our social cohesion. A man whose confidence is so shaky that he must attest to his own intelligence, malign even the most insignificant critic, scapegoat minorities and threaten the free press is to be pitied—maybe—but not trusted with power. He is very, very comfortable stoking mobs and threatening violence. His warning that there would be riots in Cleveland if he failed to get the Republican nomination—to cite just one of the thousands of ways he has transgressed basic norms this year—ought to have been enough to activate the antibodies of a healthy electorate.

Every single Republican with influence, from the local sheriff to the speaker of the house, should have stood up on their hind legs and denounced this fraud (Where are his tax returns, again?), condemned his ugly methods and scorned his flood of lies, at every stage of this process. Every Republican should have lined up for Judge Gonzalo Curiel. Gov. Chris Christie's endorsement was the first tablespoon of sewage. Sen. Jeff Sessions' was the second. The list of defilers is too long to itemize now. R.I.P. GOP.

The War On Women Is Back

Oct. 14, 2016

It's been nearly a week since the Access Hollywood tape helped to persuade key parts of the nation that Donald Trump might have a character problem. "Would you vote for a sexual predator?" asked New York Magazine. "Donald Trump Versus Hillary Clinton: Choose Your Sexual Predator" headlined The Federalist.

Yet, while rumors are flying that other shoes remain to drop, only a few women have so far come forward with stories of loutish behavior by the Republican standard bearer. Natasha Stoynoff's is the most disturbing. She alleges that she had visited Mar-a-Lago for a People magazine spread on Donald and Melania Trump (who was then pregnant). While Melania left the room to change her clothes for a photo shoot, Stoynoff recounts, Trump pushed her against the wall and "shoved his tongue down (her) throat." He backed off only when the butler announced that his wife was returning.

While it's possible that many more women will come forward with similar accounts, my guess is that Trump's actual gross conduct is probably some fraction of his claimed gross conduct. You have to apply the Trump-adjuster to every statement. Assume that 90% of what he claims—even when he's boasting of unpardonable behavior—is false.

Some of us have argued for the past year that Trump's candidacy, and his presidency, if one were to transpire, would do incalculable damage to the Republican Party and to conservative ideas.

We see one aspect of that mutilation playing out now. In 2012, Democrats invented the absurd "Republican war on women" theme. It was so over the top that it began to fray and dissolve in 2014, when Sen. Mark Udall was mocked as "Mark Uterus" for overdoing it. He lost to Cory Gardner.

But with Trump heading the Republican ticket, the war is on again. Nothing is too extreme to allege about Republicans now. Donald Trump lives down to every crude stereotype that the left has ever conjured about the right. If Clinton mad scientists attempting to create the only candidate she could defeat had concocted him in a laboratory, he could not be playing his role any better.

The damage goes far beyond an electoral defeat. Conservatives, particularly religious conservatives, who have rallied to Trump have squandered their own integrity and tainted the reputation of conservatism. They signed on for all of this when they saluted smartly and, in effect, acknowledged that all that character talk about Bill Clinton was so much gas.

Across America, college students are being instructed that "traditional" masculinity is to blame for the rape "crisis." Young men are taught that, until feminism came along, their sex had been cruel and even criminal in its understanding of and treatment of women. The website MenCanStopRape, for example, seeks to "promote an understanding of the ways in which traditional masculinity contributes to sexual assault and other forms of men's violence against women."

Conservatives saw the world differently. They argued that the sexual revolution had freed men from the responsibility to treat women respectfully. If sex was "no big deal," then the old rules no longer applied and women were left more vulnerable. Traditional masculinity, while it may have had some disadvantages, also had its virtues. Men who were raised to be gentlemen, or whose religion required sexual restraint, attempted to live by a code. They didn't always live up to their own standards, but they had standards. Gentlemen didn't cheat at sports or cheat on their wives. There were lots of rules about how to behave with women. None of them included groping or unwanted touching. They didn't use foul language in front of women or speak disparagingly about them behind their backs, either. They didn't treat women as "pieces of a—," to quote Donald Trump, or if they did, they didn't boast about it.

The sexual revolution was a project of the left, not the right. Yet the man who now represents the right is a pure product of the left's cultural inheritance. Trump, a lifelong Democrat, learned about women, he told a friend (who recounted it to PBS' Frontline), from Playboy. It shows. In fact, his critique of Bill Clinton's affair with Monica Lewinsky was that Clinton did not choose a "really beautiful woman of sophistication."

Trump is a user and abuser of people, not just women. But his disgusting behavior fits a narrative the left is spinning about sexuality and masculinity. He's the poster boy for "toxic masculinity," and every conservative who justifies or excuses him is digging the grave of conservatism even deeper.

A Little Too Much Reality in the Show?

March 21, 2018

Watching the parade of porn stars, reality TV contestants and former Playboy models lining up to lambaste the president of the United States, as well as the daily trove of stories of wife beating, naked nepotism, gambling and official corruption among his Cabinet members and White House staff, I was reminded of a story Bill Buckley once told.

He had been nominated by the Nixon administration to serve as one of our delegates to the United Nations. The FBI called around to his friends and colleagues, and one, William Rusher, groaned that he had already answered all of their questions when Buckley had been nominated for an earlier assignment. The agent replied: "I know, but it is my duty to ask whether Mr. Buckley might have done anything since 1969 to embarrass the president." The sly Rusher responded, "No, but since 1969 the Nixon administration has done a great deal to embarrass Mr. Buckley."

Imagine the FBI interviews with nominees such as Gov. Nikki Haley or Gen. James Mattis. "Have you done anything that could embarrass President Trump?" It's mind-bending. They are honorable people with stellar careers, and he is a failed casino magnate, serial adulterer, swindler of ambitious naifs (see Trump University), sexual predator and all-around louse. Yes, he's the president, but is he even capable of embarrassment?

You might say that Donald Trump isn't pretending to be a saint, and that he's tough and strong and ready to be "our" son of a b— (to paraphrase FDR's supposed description of a Latin American despot), but it's not quite that cut and dried. Trump maintains his innocence, which is where things get confusing.

Trump vehemently denies the accusations of groping and

affairs, but this week it seems that the elaborate and expensive efforts he has undertaken to conceal his behavior are unravelling a bit. The resulting prurient press party was entirely predictable.

Stormy Daniels alleges that she had an affair with Trump. At first, the world yawned. But since then we've learned that Trump's personal lawyer Michael Cohen paid her $130,000 in hush money in October 2016. (Such nice lawyers Mr. Trump hires!) That might have been a violation of campaign finance laws if Trump did not report it as an in-kind contribution. Beyond that, it reveals the contempt with which Trump treats the public. There was no affair, but Cohen had a sudden urge to make a charitable contribution to Stormy? And now Trump is suing Daniels for breach of the confidentiality agreement—in the amount of $20 million—though the official Trump position is that the agreement doesn't exist. Got that?

Some are attempting to link this to the #MeToo movement—women must speak "their truth," lawyer Gloria Allred explained—but it's a safe bet that Stormy is thinking finances, not feminism. Trump, who stresses that winning is the only virtue he upholds, should admire that.

The same cannot be said of Summer Zervos, one of the 16 women who accused Trump of groping after the release of the "Access Hollywood" tape. If you recall, Trump claimed that all of the women were lying and that he would sue them after the election. Zervos, who was a contestant on "The Apprentice," has now received the go-ahead from a judge for her lawsuit to proceed. She said he groped her. He called her a liar. She is suing for defamation. Trump's lawyers had argued that his depiction of Zervos as a liar was "political speech" and "clearly protected by the First Amendment." The judge rejected that argument, and citing the Paula Jones precedent, noted that no president is immunized against suits for purely private acts. This could open the door to sworn depositions and possible further suits.

And because character is destiny, yet another Trump acquaintance, Karen McDougal, a former Playboy model, is also attempting to invalidate her secrecy agreement. Thanks to Donald

Trump, we've learned that the gossip magazines have a practice called "catch and kill" for stories they want to suppress. The parent company of the National Enquirer apparently performed this service for Trump, paying McDougal $150,000 for the rights to her story.

Nevertheless, McDougal seems ready to tell her tale, and Daniels will tell hers (including allegations of threats emanating from Trump world). And perhaps, just perhaps, as they settle in this weekend to watch "60 Minutes," the party of family values will wonder whether they really wanted to sign up for all this.

The Meaning of Ryan's Departure

April 13, 2018

I've always felt a kinship with Paul Ryan. Maybe it's the fact that we are both Jack Kemp acolytes. Maybe I have a soft spot for upright family men who are attracted to public policy by the desire to do good. Maybe I love conservative wonks. But Paul Ryan's fate over the past several years is as good an indication as any of how far our politics have fallen.

Ryan's departure will not be mourned by Democrats or Trump loyalists. The Democrats caricatured Ryan as the goon throwing Granny in her wheelchair off a cliff. They actually ran TV ads with a Ryan lookalike. Barack Obama singled him out for scorn at a White House meeting, claiming later that he was unaware Ryan was in the front row.

You might suppose that that would be enough to make Ryan a conservative hero, but life is often unjust, and when Donald Trump came along, Ryan found himself a sudden symbol of the reviled "Republican establishment." Though the anti-Ryan vitriol faded after Steve Bannon's defenestration, he continued to be viewed with suspicion by the talk radio crowd and other arms of Trump Inc.

This was his reward for attempting to drag his party, and the country, toward a grown-up reckoning with our debt. Nearly single-handedly, Paul Ryan had managed to put tackling entitlements on the national agenda. As chairman of the budget committee, he convinced his colleagues to endorse modest entitlement reform. As he kept trying to explain, making incremental reforms now—with no changes for current beneficiaries or those in their 50s—can prevent drastic shortfalls and extreme benefit cuts that will be necessary in just 16 years, when Social Security is depleted. The outlook is even worse for Medicare and Medicaid.

But Donald Trump arrived on scene with the supposedly blinding insight that changes to entitlements are unpopular. Well, no kidding. He promised never to touch Medicare and Social Security—not even to ensure their future solvency. And so, the responsible, future-oriented Paul Ryan found himself governing with a backward-looking, whistling past the-graveyard president.

Even leaving aside the moral compromises that an alliance with Donald Trump necessitated, Ryan and the party he helped to lead also lost its compass on Ryan's own signature issue: fiscal responsibility.

Tax reform may have been overdue, but it would have been nice if the party that fulminated about the dangers of deficits in the Obama years had found anything at all to cut—particularly as the economy is growing and unemployment is low. Instead, the budget and the tax bill combined will leave us with a federal budget deficit in excess of $1 trillion in 2020 and beyond. Congressional Budget Office Director Keith Hall said that federal debt "is projected to be on a steadily rising trajectory throughout the decade." Under Republican guidance, the federal deficit will be roughly double what it was in the final year of the Obama administration. That is the reality of Speaker Ryan's tenure in the age of Trump.

It is often suggested that Trump has much to teach the Republican Party about the importance of the white working class and about the centrality of nationalism to Republican success.

But just as with entitlement reform, it's one thing to say a thing is popular and quite another to say that it's right.

What has Trump taught? That trade wars are the way to improve the lives of the working class? They *are* popular, at least with Republicans. A Politico/Morning Consult poll found that 65% of Republicans favored Trump's steel and aluminum tariffs. But if Republicans believe, as the overwhelming majority do, that tariffs are stupid and dangerous, then it would seem obvious that they have something to teach the president rather than the other way around.

I can't say for sure, but I suspect that Paul Ryan's diagnosis of what ails America is pretty similar to my own. We are not behaving as responsible adults. Our greatest political challenge is out-of-control debt. Our greatest social challenges are declining families, increasing dependency and eroding social cohesion. The debt could have been addressed by government. The other trends continue to degrade our culture, our economy and our personal lives. And the ascension of Trumpian politics—slashing, mendacious, corrupt and polarizing—aggravates everything that was already going wrong.

Paul Ryan didn't belong in Trump world. So much the worse for us.

Being Decent

June 22, 2018

Not too long ago, I returned to my parked car and found a sheet of paper on the windshield bearing an expletive-laden message. The anonymous poster had obviously gone to some effort to make these flyers on his home computer—complete with color cartoon figures and such. It let me know what an (obscenity) I was. My sin was having parked my car a tiny bit over the white line. I confess. I'm guilty. The garage was full of empty spaces, mind you, and it was only a few inches, but still, it was wrong. But did it require that response? If he had to vent his rage, couldn't he have left a note saying "It's inconsiderate to park over the white line"? My offense seems to have been merely an excuse. This person, clearly overflowing with hostility toward his fellow men, had preprinted these vulgar missives, and delivered them to everyone who offended him.

Is it my imagination or has the tone of the internet seeped into daily life? People often suggest that Twitter's cruelty and misanthropy are unique to the format. Announcing that he was deleting Twitter from his phone, Andrew Sullivan advised: "Social media has turned journalism into junk, has promoted addictive addlement in our brains, is wrecking our democracy, and slowly replacing life with pseudo-life."

The comments sections of websites are sewers, some have suggested, because they're anonymous. I used to think that. Now I'm not so sure. While anonymity clearly unleashes some of the darker sides of human nature (which is one of the reasons mobs are so dangerous), and while real life is somewhat more civilized than "pseudo-life," the indecency is now quite open in our politics, our entertainment and, as noted in the car story (and other stories I could tell), in daily life.

What happened when Samantha Bee used the C-word with reference to Ivanka Trump? She ought to have been greeted with shocked silence. Instead, she got applause. When Robert De Niro unloaded the F-bomb on Donald Trump, he got a standing ovation at the Tony Awards. These cultural figures are clearly not thinking things through. If they object to Donald Trump's vulgarity and norm violating, they forfeit their standing by responding exactly in kind. If you find him offensive, maybe you shouldn't emulate him.

Almost exactly 64 years ago, the subject of decency became a national showstopper. At the Army/McCarthy hearings, attorney Joseph Welch, representing the Army, punctured the pretensions of Roy Cohn, Sen. Joe McCarthy's aide, by demanding that he release the senator's list of 130 subversives "before sundown." Cohn couldn't, as Welch well knew. The list wasn't real. (There were communists in the State Department, but McCarthy threw wild charges in all directions and tainted the entire anti-Communist cause.) When Welch raised the matter of Roy Cohn's use of taxpayer dollars to wine and dine his friend, and Cohn's abuse of his government post to pester the Army to afford his friend special treatment, McCarthy responded (as he usually did) with an accusation of his own. Instead of answering the criticism, he did something die-hard Trump fans would love: He leveled a new accusation, this time against a lawyer in Welch's firm, who had been a member of the left-wing National Lawyers Guild. Welch responded, "Until this moment, senator, I think I never really gauged your cruelty or your recklessness. ... Have you no sense of decency, sir?"

McCarthy didn't. And in the 1950s, it proved his undoing. Nor did Roy Cohn, who went on to a lucrative, if dodgy, career marked by corner cutting and allegations of professional misconduct (he was disbarred in 1986). His most significant role in history may well have been taking a young Donald Trump under his wing and modeling the "never back down, never apologize" style we've come to know so well.

This entire administration, taking its cue from the president, has engaged in indecency on an unprecedented scale. We've elected the boarding school bully. Just a day before the president reversed his position on tearing children from their parents' arms, Corey Lewandowski, confronted with the story of a 10-year-old child with Down syndrome forcibly separated from her mother at the border, scoffed, "Womp, womp." That's the Trump spirit.

Republicans keep mostly silent about Trump's assaults on basic morality because they fear his popularity with their voters. It's small and cowardly. But the Democrats have nothing to fear from modeling basic integrity, civility and fidelity to truth. They should try it.

Bully Wannabees

Feb. 13, 2020

Matt Schlapp, chairman of the American Conservative (cough) Union, which hosts the annual CPAC conference, tweeted that he was disinviting Mitt Romney from the confab this year because he "could not guarantee his physical safety" after the senator voted to convict Donald Trump in the impeachment trial.

A number of commentators on the left have responded to this by dismissing CPAC attendees as a bunch of brown shirts. I don't think that's right. I spoke at CPAC in 2018 and courted trouble by criticizing both Roy Moore and Donald Trump for their documented histories of sexual misconduct, as well as CPAC itself for inviting the niece of Marine Le Pen, Marion Marechal Le Pen, a right-wing nativist from France.

I was jeered; it's true. So what? I've been booed before (though, admittedly, not before a conservative audience). I didn't feel threatened or intimidated. Some in the crowd even offered a thumbs up. It was Schlapp, observing from a control room, who apparently decided to have me ushered out by beefy guards. Thus was born the "Charen had to be escorted out of CPAC under guard" story.

It occurs to me, now that Schlapp is playing the bullyboy with Mitt Romney, that he enjoys the whiff of menace. It is he, not the audience, that is dangerous. But, of course, when leaders stir grievances and hint that mob violence is possible, they tend to get the followers they deserve.

Schlapp is representative of the bully chic that has come into fashion in Trump's party. Senator Martha McSally snapped at a CNN reporter, calling him a liberal hack. Anyone can lose one's cool, but instead of apologizing when the moment passed,

McSally used her lapse of manners as a publicity opportunity on Fox News and was fundraising off it before you could say "Trumpian."

Secretary of State Michael Pompeo, who graduated first in his class at West Point and served honorably as a tank platoon leader in the U.S. Army, has sniffed the air and decided that behaving completely unprofessionally is fine if you are subjected to tough questions from reporters. When Mary Louise Kelly of NPR asked whether he had stood up for Ambassador Marie Yovanovitch, Pompeo surrendered to his inner toddler. He ended the interview abruptly. Not content with that, he then called Kelly into his private office and screamed at her, demanding, "Do you think Americans care about f— Ukraine?"

That alone would have been bad enough. But Pompeo wasn't finished. Calling an assistant, he asked for an unmarked map of the world and then challenged Kelly to identify Ukraine. She did. Nevertheless, Pompeo put out the story that she had pointed to Bangladesh. Okaaay. Kelly has a master's degree in European studies from Cambridge, and has reported from Ukraine. You decide.

But why does the secretary of state keep unmarked world maps in his office anyway? Wonder how it would go if he challenged his boss to point out key sites?

Members of Congress loyal to Trump seem to take notes from mob movies. When former Trump lawyer/fixer Michael Cohen was preparing to testify before the House Oversight and Government Reform Committee, Rep. Matt Gaetz tweeted out a threat: "Hey @MichaelCohen212—Do your wife & father-in-law know about your girlfriends? Maybe tonight would be a good time for that chat. I wonder if she'll remain faithful when you're in prison. She's about to learn a lot."

During the president's impeachment trial, Senator Rand Paul repeatedly attempted to get the chief justice of the United States to read aloud the alleged name of the whistleblower. When Justice Roberts demurred, Rand Paul pronounced it himself on the Senate floor. Whistleblowers are shielded from retaliation by law, and under the circumstances, with death threats flying, revealing his or her identity could be called retaliation. In any case, it's a thuggish message to any future whistleblowers: Nice career you've got there, be a shame if anything were to happen to it.

Never to be outdone, the first son was ready with a cloddish put down of Mitt Romney. Photoshopping the senator in ill-fitting jeans, Donald Trump Jr. sneered, "Mom jeans, because you're a p——."

Trump Smashes the Right's Ability to Police Itself

May 22, 2020

Among dozens of addled tweets from the commander in chief over the past few days, one in particular deserves pausing over because it demonstrates not just the weak-mindedness of our president but also the way his leadership is sabotaging conservatism.

Trump retweeted a post featuring disgraced columnist Michelle Malkin, who complained about being silenced on social media. Trump responded: "The radical left is in total command & control of Facebook, Instagram, Twitter and Google. The administration is working to remedy this illegal situation. Stay tuned, and send names & events. Thank you Michelle!"

In the name of standing up for aggrieved conservatives, Trump soils the brand. First, a detail. The "radical left" is not in control of those outlets, and even if it were, they are private entities and therefore perfectly free to make their own judgments about content. There is nothing "illegal" about it. If the administration *were* working to "remedy" the situation, that is what would be illegal. Another detail: Trump has 19.7 million followers on Instagram, 26.7 million on Facebook and 80 million on Twitter. Perhaps what keeps him so popular is his audience's inexhaustible appetite for whining.

The woman Trump thanked is a columnist and social media entrepreneur who was a respected member of the conservative commentariat—emphasis on the past tense. In the past two years, she has been shunned by respectable conservative outlets. She is no longer welcome at CPAC. The Young America's Foundation has dropped her, and the Daily Wire and National Review discontinued her syndicated column.

The occasion for the deplatforming was Malkin's swan dive into the right-wing fever swamps. In 2017, she endorsed alt-right candidate Paul Nehlen ("Paul Nehlen slams … corporate open-borders elites!"), and contributed to the VDARE website which frequently hosts white nationalists, racists and anti-Semites.

Her most grotesque relationship though, and the one that got her booted from the Young America's Foundation, was with a group calling themselves "groypers," led by a 21-year-old YouTube host named Nick Fuentes. To get a sense of just how loathsome this figure is, have a look at this video in which he wonders, grinning, about whether 6 million "cookies" could really be baked in ovens and how the "math doesn't add up." Holocaust jokes. How droll. Fuentes, you will not be shocked to learn, is one of the "very fine people" who marched with neo-Nazis at the 2017 Unite the Right rally in Charlottesville. Remember Pepe the Frog? He's their mascot. He described the mass murder in an El Paso Walmart as an "act of desperation." Turning Point USA is too tame for his tastes, and his group has lately been heckling speakers like Ben Shapiro, Dan Crenshaw and even Donald Trump Jr.

Yet, Malkin has declared herself the "mother of groypers" and called them "good kids." When she was rebuked by mainstream conservatives, she declared her allegiances proudly:

"They want me to disavow Nick Fuentes and VDARE and Peter Brimelow and Faith Goldy and Gavin McInnes and the Proud Boys and Steve King and Laura Loomer and on and on."

"They" did want that, but now Trump has vitiated that work by praising Malkin. The thing Trump retweeted was not actually a Malkin post, but a tweet of Malkin speaking to the Western Conservative Summit. "America First Clips" is a feed for one of Fuentes's outlets. Naturally, Fuentes is gloating.

Trump defenders will no doubt protest that Trump knew nothing of Malkin's descent into neo-Nazi land. But that's no excuse. In fact, Trump probably did not know much about those he praised, either Malkin or, by extension, Fuentes. But he has a duty to know. Yes, he's an indolent ignoramus, but guess what, the taxpayers are paying for a huge staff. He has people who can check. He doesn't use them because he doesn't care. His moral reasoning is primitive. If you are pro-Trump, no matter what else you are (a murderous dictator, a racist troll), you're fine in his book. Loutish protesters harass a TV journalist using the F words ("fake news" and, you know, the other one), and Trump proclaims them "great people." He has no objective moral standards. Everything is about him. On a scale of moral reasoning, he is subzero. But the world of conservative opinion-shapers does still attempt, however weakly, to maintain some guard rails. With every passing day of Donald Trump's leadership, those standards crumble a bit more.

LOL: Some Things Do Matter After All

June 12, 2020

We thought it was a fixed feature of our new era. We thought that objective reality didn't matter anymore, if it even existed at all. We thought we were so entrapped by our information silos that nothing could penetrate. "LOL. Nothing matters" ran the Twitter meme.

What we've learned in the past two weeks is that we were wrong. Reality reasserts itself. Minds can change. Just weeks ago, Black Lives Matter was regarded as a fringe movement, a response to a real problem perhaps, but a vastly exaggerated one. Today, the slogan emblazons 16th Street in front of the White House. As Politico's Tim Alberta reports, in 2014, after Eric Garner was choked by police, only 33% of Americans believed that blacks were more likely to be mistreated by police than others. Only 26% of whites thought so. Today, 57% of Americans, including 49% of whites, believe police are more likely to use force against African Americans. This week, the 2012 Republican nominee for president marched in solidarity with Black Lives Matter in Washington, D.C. The last two-term Republican president released a statement using the term "systemic racism," which curled the toes of some right-wing commentators but comports with the views of more than 80% of Americans. An eyebrow-raising 29% of Republicans say President Donald Trump has "mostly increased" racial tensions, along with 92% of Democrats and 73% of independents. The conservative Drudge Report website, once a redoubt of Trump enthusiasm, hawked "Justice for George Floyd" T-shirts.

After the president tweeted, "When the looting starts, the shooting starts," Trump's approval rating among independents dropped 10 points, from 40 to 30%. His handling of the Floyd murder aftermath has cost him even among Republicans, 83% of whom rated him favorably in May, compared with 90% in April. White evangelical Christians, the constituency that inspired Trump's Bible semaphore in front of St. John's Church, have also soured a bit on the "law and order" president. In May, 62% rated him favorably, down from 77% in April.

The country is executing a dramatic turn on questions of racial justice. That vile video of depraved police suffocating a handcuffed man has penetrated our armor-plated opinion silos. Coming after other high-profile outrages, it has ignited a movement. And while some have allowed the moment to overwhelm their judgment, calling for example, not just to reform the police but to "defund" the police (which will. not. happen.), it will be interesting to see where this leaves the Republican Party.

Have a look at this email I received from Amanda Chase, the first announced Republican candidate for Virginia governor in 2021. "Help me save the Robert E. Lee statue!" she pleads. That's what the Republican Party of Virginia now stands for?

One extremist does not a party define. True enough. But the Republican Party of Virginia previously nominated Corey Stewart for a U.S. Senate seat. He defended the Unite the Right rally in Charlottesville, and had previously made a name for himself by defending Confederate monuments, or "taking back our heritage" as he put it, which is odd because Stewart grew up in Minnesota, the first state to send volunteers to quell the rebellion in 1861.

The Republican Party of Alabama nominated Roy Moore for the U.S. Senate. Aside from his predation on young teenage girls, Moore was an enthusiastic "birther." The Republican Party of Oregon has nominated Jo Rae Perkins, a promoter of the QAnon conspiracy, for the U.S. Senate.

The list goes on and on. The alt-right and the nutty right have made inroads into the Republican Party with only occasional pushback, as when the Republican caucus denied committee assignments to defeated Iowa Rep. Steve ("When did white supremacist become offensive?") King.

The party of Lincoln has assented to the pardon of Joe Arpaio. It found nothing much to say about the smearing of Mexicans as drug dealers and rapists. When the president said an Indiana-born judge could not be fair because his parents were from Mexico, one prominent Republican, Paul Ryan, called that "classic racism." He's gone now. When the president told four darker-skinned members of Congress to "go back where you came from," (three were born here), the Republican Party had nothing.

Most Republicans are not extremists or conspiracists or racists, but they look at their shoes and kick the dirt when those elements succeed in their party. Now the country is reevaluating questions of policing and race, finding previously elusive agreement on the need for reform, and exposing just how lost the Republican Party has become.

Why This Pro-Life Conservative Is Voting for Biden

Aug. 28, 2020

Since I announced publicly that I will be voting for Joe Biden in November, I've received a few communications from puzzled readers. "How can you, a supposedly pro-life woman, support someone who believes in killing babies?"

I will try to respond for the sake of those who, like me, find themselves alienated from the Republican Party despite some policy agreements with the Trump administration.

I have been pro-life my entire adult life. I haven't changed. I continue to find the practice abhorrent and will persist in trying to persuade others. While I would prefer to vote for someone who upholds the right to life, I've never believed that electing presidents who agree with me will lead to dramatic changes in abortion law, nor is the law itself the only way to discourage abortion. The number of abortions has been declining steadily since 1981. It dropped during Republican presidencies and during Democratic presidencies, and now stands below the rate in 1973, when Roe v. Wade was decided and when abortion was illegal in 44 states.

It's wrong to take innocent life. But other things are immoral too. It's also wrong to swindle people, to degrade and demonize, to incite violence, to bully, and while we're at it, to steal, to bear false witness, to commit adultery and to covet.

Donald Trump is a daily, even hourly, assault on the very idea of morality, even as he obliterates truth. His influence is like sulfuric acid on our civic bonds. His cruelty is contagious. Remember how he mocked a handicapped reporter in 2016? His defenders either denied the obvious facts, or insisted that, while

Trump himself might be "politically incorrect," his supporters wouldn't be influenced by that aspect of his character.

Alas, they are. Consider the incredibly moving moment during the Democratic National Convention when young Braydon Harrington, who struggles with stuttering, introduced Joe Biden. That night, an Atlantic editor with the same affliction tweeted: "This is what stutterers face every day. I'm in awe of Braydon's courage and resolve." That prompted Austin Ruse, author of "The Catholic Case for Trump," to tweet in response: "W-w-w-w-w-w-what?"

It isn't just a matter of style. At Donald Trump's order, thousands of children, including hundreds under the age of 4, were forcibly separated from their parents at the border. Pro-lifers are tender-hearted about the most vulnerable members of society. So, images like this must stir something. Separating children from their parents is a barbaric act. In the crush of outrages over the past three and a half years, it has gotten swallowed up, but the horror of what was done in our name should never be forgotten.

All of this is familiar to Trump supporters, but they will vote for him because they believe that the left is far worse.

Rep. Matt Gaetz, R-Fla., characteristically subtle, claimed at the RNC that Biden and Democrats will, "disarm you, empty the prisons, lock you in your home, and invite MS-13 to live next door. And the defunded police aren't on their way."

Funny, but I could have sworn that the Democratic Party nominated Joe Biden last week, not Alexandria Ocasio-Cortez.

Look, there are extremists on the left, and the Democratic Party has a weakness for not calling them out. Democrats do the truth and themselves no favors by attempting to gloss over the looting, arson and vandalism that have persisted in Portland, Chicago and other cities throughout the summer.

But it's dishonest, and frankly, a bit hysterical, to attempt to hang every sin of the left around Joe Biden's neck. He's no radical, and the party that nominated him showed that its centrist core was stronger than its extremist wing.

In the wake of renewed violence following yet another horrific police shooting, this time in Kenosha, Wisconsin, Biden issued a humane statement expressing deep sympathy for Jacob Blake and his family, outrage at what happened and also condemnation of violence, saying: "burning down communities is not protest, it's needless violence … That's wrong." Biden struck exactly the right tone.

The argument that the left is worse doesn't persuade me. Strange as it is to write those words after 30-plus years as a conservative columnist, I have to say that when you compare the state of the two major parties today, the Republicans are more frightening.

It is the Republican Party that has *officially* become a personality cult, declaring that it will not adopt a platform but will simply follow whatever Trump dictates. And it is the Republican Party that now opens its arms to adherents of a deranged and dangerous new cult called QAnon. The FBI has designated QAnon a domestic terror threat, yet minority leader Kevin McCarthy has committed to providing committee assignments to Marjorie Taylor Greene, should she be elected in November.

There is putrefaction where the Republican Party's essence should be, and appointing pro-life judges cannot mask the stench. So, this conservative is voting for the Democrats. Will the GOP reform? I hope so. But my priority isn't trying to heal the Republican Party. It's trying to heal the country.

Trump's Republican Party

Oct. 8, 2020

Kelly Loeffler looked like a standard-issue Republican when she was appointed senator from Georgia in December 2019. She came from a super-rich family (like plenty of Democrats as well), she was pro-gun, anti-immigration and pro-business. Originally pro-choice, her position on abortion evolved in time for her to be accepted by pro-life gatekeepers.

Once in Washington, D.C., though, Loeffler quickly got with the program. She described the impeachment of the president as a "circus" and lambasted Mitt Romney for even voting to call witnesses, whom she was sure would "slander @realDonald Trump." Now, she's encouraging hero worship of Trump, tweeting: "COVID stood NO chance against @realDonaldTrump."

This is servile, particularly at a moment when he is literally endangering others' lives. When she appeared, maskless and within inches of others, indoors at the White House announcement for Amy Coney Barrett, she not only endangered her own health and the health of her loved ones, she became a soldier in the disinformation war Trump is fighting to dissuade Americans from taking the threat seriously.

Only yesterday, Republicans were livid that President Barack Obama downplayed the threat from terrorism. I recall being appalled that no leading American statesman attended a Paris rally following the 2015 massacre at Charlie Hebdo headquarters, though European heads of state were there, along with Israel's Benjamin Netanyahu and even the Palestinian Authority's Mahmoud Abbas. Attorney General Eric Holder was in Paris at the time, but he skipped the march. Republicans fervently believed that failure to confront terrorist threats to the nation was malfeasance at best and betrayal at worst.

Yet now, to compensate for the inability of the current president to manage a two-car funeral, we are asked to believe that declining to confront the threat from a virus is neither malfeasance nor betrayal but instead some sort of macho heroism. Tomi Lahren of Fox Nation tweeted that Joe Biden should carry a purse to go with his face mask. The fawning Rep. Matt Gaetz tweeted: "President Trump won't have to recover from COVID. COVID will have to recover from President Trump." And Fox News host Greg Gutfeld said this:

"Maybe it's a flaw of Trump ... he didn't hide from the virus. The reason he didn't hide from the virus is he didn't want America to hide from the virus. If he was going to ask America to get back to work, right? ... So he took the risk, he got the virus, but he was doing it for us."

He suffered for our sins? Yep, that's Trump all over.

Let me offer a few more flashbulb glimpses of the state of the GOP today. A quick glance at the Trump fans who gathered outside Walter Reed Hospital over the weekend revealed one holding a sign mentioning QAnon (there may well have been others), and another with a placard cheerily emblazoned "Super-spreader event."

Flash: Greg Abbott, Republican governor of Texas, apparently abandoning several common-sense measures to cope with the coronavirus like expanding early voting, has now announced that he will limit the number of ballot drop boxes to one per county. Texas has 254 counties with an average of about 114,000 people in each. But, of course, they vary in size. The single ballot drop box in Loving County will only have to handle the county's 169 residents. The box in Harris County, home to Houston, will have to accommodate 4.7 million. They better get a big box.

Flash: Sen. Ron Johnson, who has tested positive for the coronavirus (along with Sens. Mike Lee and Thom Tillis), said he remains opposed to mask mandates because "while masks can reduce the risk of infection, they're not a cure-all." Is Johnson also opposed to food safety mandates, because while they decrease the incidence of poisoning, they're not a cure-all?

Flash: Sen. Pat Toomey, one of the last semi-sincere conservatives, bows out. He never wavered from his free trade principles and opposed Trump's revised NAFTA treaty because it flouted those principles. He joins the 40% of elected Republicans in Washington who have resigned or retired since 2017.

Flash: The National Republican Congressional Committee has targeted a New Jersey freshman Democrat with ads aimed at linking him to what QAnon supporters believe is a Satanic, cannibalistic, child-abuse conspiracy backed by Hollywood and Democrats. The grounds? Rep. Tom Malinowski supposedly opposed expanding a sex offender registry. He denies this, but frankly, even if he had, it's a totally reasonable position to adopt. I've written about the gross miscarriages of justice those registries can cause. The NRCC is not a fringe political action committee. It's the official campaign arm of the Republican caucus in the House of Representatives, and it now issues official statements that read like supermarket tabloids. "Rep. Tom Malinoski lobbied to protect sexual predators."

This GOP is inhospitable to conservatives (see former Speaker of the House Paul Ryan among many others), moderates (see John Kasich) and people of decency and courage (see Mitt Romney). Rather than purging its ranks of kooks and conspiracists, it welcomes and courts them. Rather than fight fair, it seeks to win by keeping people from the polls.

America needs a sane, serious, humane, center-right party that aims to persuade, not to dominate. This GOP is not it.

Decency RIP

July 2, 2021

Sen. Mitt Romney appeared on Jake Tapper's CNN show last weekend, and for a few brief minutes, I felt transported to a saner world. Asked about the gross things some on the right are saying about Gen. Mark Milley, he responded that "Gen. Milley is a person of extraordinary accomplishment and personal character and a brilliant man." Asked about continuing allegations from the former president and his enablers that the election was stolen, Romney didn't hesitate to call it "the big lie."

On substance, Romney was rock solid. He opposes government efforts to dictate what is taught in schools. He supports spending $1.2 trillion on roads, bridges, rail, air, water pipes, broadband and more, but when Tapper noted that the American Society of Civil Engineers wants to spend an additional $800 billion, Romney responded politely but deftly: "Well, I must admit that I do pay a lot of attention to the engineers, but, of course, they're paid based upon how much we spend in their arena." Spoken like someone who wasn't born yesterday.

Romney knew the infrastructure bill in detail. He praised President Joe Biden and Secretary of State Antony Blinken. He differed with Democrats about social spending and taxes. He stated unequivocally that the election was free and fair. In short, he was completely out of step with modern "conservatism" and the GOP.

Some said that the permanent change former President Donald Trump would effect in the Republican Party would be a heightened attention to the needs of the working class. That may or may not materialize. Some Republicans are making noises about being a "worker's party," but there doesn't appear to be anything concrete there yet.

No, the biggest post-Trump change is the eager embrace of indecency. On his Fox show, Tucker Carlson played a clip of Milley explaining that he thinks it's important to hear various points of view (even critical race theory). At the conclusion of the clip, Carlson spat, "He's not just a pig; he's stupid!"

The host of a widely viewed TV show should be, if not a model of decorum, at least not a foam-flecked fulminator. That's part of what it means to live in a civilized society. And certainly, a much-decorated general, the chairman of the Joint Chiefs of Staff, is entitled to respect for his service to the country. *Every* member of the military deserves to be honored for his or her service. Or, if that's too much to manage, how about not grossly insulted? And this from a self-styled conservative? Didn't conservatives once fume about someone in the Clinton White House saying something disrespectful to an officer? Didn't they mock former President Barack Obama over a coffee cup salute?

The 2021 conservatives clearly don't respect the military or the police (see Jan. 6) if it's inconvenient. While dissing decorated officers, these new conservatives eagerly embrace war criminals. Fox News has campaigned on their behalf, and Trump pardoned several. When Trump suggested targeting the children of terrorists, or told police to rough up suspects, or denied raping a woman because "she's not my type," or intimated that a deceased Democratic politician was in hell, Republicans nodded along.

Nikki Haley, who once calculated that the best path to political prominence in the GOP was to remove the Confederate flag from the South Carolina Capitol grounds following the brutal massacre of African American churchgoers, has now figured out that basic decency is the road to irrelevance. In 2015, she explained movingly that "the flag is a deeply offensive symbol of a brutally oppressive past."

No more of that. Campaigning in Iowa recently, she told the audience that "Republicans are too nice. I wear heels. It's not for a fashion statement. I use them for kicking. But I always kick with a smile." Haley has probably set some sort of record for flushing her own dignity down the toilet in record time. She's sensing the mood of the Republican base. It's ugly, so she's diving in.

Do you remember—eons or five years ago—when it was considered beneath contempt to attack a politician's family? Bring the heat for the man in the arena, but by all that is holy, leave his wife and kids out of it? It seems antique now. When one of the Biden family dogs passed away a couple of weeks ago, a National Review writer tweeted: "Champ Biden dies, Major lives on. The Biden family tragedy in miniature."

Mocking a family when they've lost a beloved pet, which was the way some on Twitter interpreted this, would have been tasteless and cruel. But this was much more sinister. The implication was that Biden's "good son," Beau, had died while his brother, Hunter, lived on. Who does that? And especially those who call themselves conservative and constantly rant about threats to civilization. How can they not see that undermining basic civility and decency is itself an attack on civilization?

Well, at least we have Romney, and a few more, to remind Republicans of what they once were and could be again.

What We Lost When the GOP Lost Itself

Oct. 1, 2021

In the typhoon of congressional brinkmanship we've witnessed this week, one detail caught my eye that could easily have been lost in the gales. A group of 35 Republican senators signed a letter to Majority Leader Chuck Schumer and Finance Committee Chairman Ron Wyden about an aspect of the House reconciliation bill that they find disturbing.

"As you know, current marriage penalties occur when a household's overall tax bill increases due to a couple marrying and filing taxes jointly. ... Unfortunately, despite its original rollout as part of the 'American Families Plan,' the current draft of the reconciliation bill takes an existing marriage penalty in the Earned Income Tax Credit (EITC) and makes it significantly worse. This is not the only marriage penalty created or worsened by the partisan bill."

For the record, I think this objection is completely sound. If there's one thing the social science literature is virtually unanimous about, it's that two parents are better than one. And while marriage isn't essential to ensuring that a child grows up in a stable home—some cohabiting parents stay together for decades, and some single parents provide very stable homes—the association is extremely strong. Anyone concerned about child poverty needs to be concerned about marriage. Kids who grow up in two-parent families have a poverty rate of 7.5%, compared with 36.5% of those raised in single-parent homes.

It's not just poverty. Kids raised in stable homes without a revolving door of new adult partners for their parents and new stepsiblings (actual or de facto) for themselves are healthier physically and psychologically. They are less likely to struggle in school, get in trouble with the law, engage in risky behaviors or get depressed and commit suicide. The United States has the dubious distinction of having more children living with only one adult (23%) than any other nation on earth. A Pew survey of 130 countries found that the global average is 7%.

This link between marriage and good outcomes for children is so robust that scholars across the political divide agree on it, though they may differ on what to do about it, or about whether it is even possible to do anything about the growing percentage of children growing up in single-parent homes.

Government efforts to encourage marriage, such as those undertaken by the George W. Bush administration, were well-intentioned flops. They included funding for programs that offered counseling for new mothers on the virtues of marriage as well as couples therapy and public service announcements featuring celebrities. The divorce/unwed parenting numbers didn't respond. (Divorce has been trending down since its peak in 1980, but the percentage of children growing up in single-parent homes has not decreased due to the rise of unwed childbearing.)

The government's failure to affect matrimony should surprise exactly no one. For one thing, the programs didn't last long, but that's probably for the best. A behavior as complex as choosing whether or not to marry is unlikely to be affected by government encouragement. It's the same with other behaviors. Remember the "President's Challenge" to eat healthy and exercise more? That was another Bush initiative. These hortatory programs have a long pedigree. President Dwight Eisenhower founded the President's Council on Youth Fitness in 1956. Rates of obesity have stubbornly increased in every decade since.

This is not to say that we should throw up our hands. Cultural change happens all the time. Just consider how much we've been able to curb drunk driving over the past 25 years due to changing mores and the activism of civil society groups like Mothers Against Drunk Driving.

But there is one huge thing the government can do: stop making things worse. Every tax or safety net-related marriage penalty should be sandblasted out of the code. The Republican senators are completely right about this. If it means the programs cost more, so be it. It's worth it.

This is precisely the kind of perspective we need a healthy conservative party to advance. We need a party that is focused on the importance of the mediating institutions in society—families, churches, schools and community organizations—rather than simply on individuals and government. This is too frequently a blind spot for Democrats.

But today's Republican Party has forfeited the benefit of the doubt. You need a certain moral standing to be taken seriously on matters like the marriage penalty. You rely on voters to believe that you are at least partly motivated by good policy. But when Sen. Mitch McConnell cynically filibusters a bill to raise the debt ceiling to cover bills his party helped to rack up; when Republicans open their ranks to the likes of Reps. Paul Gosar, Lauren Boebert and Marjorie Taylor Greene; when the party thwarts basic public health measures like vaccines and masks; and when the party closes ranks around former President Donald Trump by blocking an independent commission to investigate the Jan. 6 riot, well, people will doubt your bona fides.

Republicans are also endangering our democracy with their embrace of Trump's election fraud fantasy. That's the most urgent threat. But it's also a loss for this country that the Republican Party is discrediting conservatism, because we can't do without it.

Dr. Oz Quacks the Code of Republican Politics

Dec. 3, 2021

Sean Parnell, the Trump-anointed candidate for Senate in Pennsylvania, dropped out of the race a week ago after a custody hearing that featured lurid details of his relationship with his ex-wife. Laurie Snell alleged that Parnell had struck her, choked her, left her by the side of the road and hit one of their sons hard enough to leave a welt on the boy's back. Parnell countered that she had invented all of it.

Custody battles are infamous for exaggerated accusations and heated denials, and it's difficult for outsiders to know whom to believe and how much. But Parnell's comments off the witness stand didn't burnish his credibility. Appearing on Fox Nation, for example, Parnell opined, "I feel like the whole 'happy wife, happy life' nonsense has done nothing but raise one generation of woman tyrants after the next." He wasn't finished. "Now there's an entire generation of men that don't want to put up with the BS of a high-maintenance, narcissistic woman." Well. Someone seems to be dealing with anger issues. The would-be—er, rather, won't-be—senator concluded with a short sermon on biology: "From an evolutionary standpoint, it used to be, you know, women were attracted to your strength because you could defend them from dinosaurs." Where does the GOP find these geniuses?

Well, this one was one of the crops cultivated by Fox News. Parnell served, apparently honorably, in Afghanistan and wrote a book about his war experiences, but since his discharge, he has sought advancement mostly through public speaking. Becoming famous is a stand-alone career goal these days. Parnell was Diamond and Silk with testosterone. Fox and other right-wing media elevated him. He ran once for Congress—unsuccessfully. That's the whole resume. But Parnell caught the eye of the dauphin, Donald Trump Jr., who told Trump Sr. about him and voila, he was on his way to the U.S. Senate ... until the judge in the above-mentioned hearing awarded full custody of his three children to his ex-wife.

So, with the departure of the dinosaur slayer, the field was open for another clown. We'll come to Dr. Oz in a moment, but first, consider Chris Sununu.

Sununu is the very popular three-term governor of New Hampshire whom Mitch McConnell had been begging to enter the Senate race in 2022. Polls had shown Sununu running 7 points ahead of sitting Sen. Maggie Hassan. But on Nov. 9, he announced that he would forgo a Senate bid in favor of running for a fourth term as New Hampshire governor. Sununu may not be your cup of tea as a leader—he isn't mine in all respects—but he has a record. He's for low taxes, state support for substance abusers, the death penalty, school choice, abortion rights, constitutional carry and LGBT-friendly measures such as permitting a nonbinary designation on driver's licenses. Before running for office, he worked as an environmental engineer and then as CEO of a ski resort that employed about 700 people. All told, a serious person with a checkable resume. Unlike some other northeast Republican governors, Sununu endorsed Donald Trump for reelection.

That Sununu, a solid, substantive politician (with an asterisk for his Trump endorsement), has no interest in an easy glidepath to the United States Senate speaks volumes about the state of the national GOP.

That brings us to Dr. Mehmet Oz. Unlike Parnell, Oz has impressive professional credentials and career accomplishments. He's a cardiothoracic surgeon and professor at Columbia University's College of Physicians and Surgeons. He holds degrees from Harvard and the University of Pennsylvania (both the business and medical schools).

Oz could be at the pinnacle of America's professional class—

respected, well-compensated, privileged to devote his career to caring for others, and teaching rising generations to do the same.

But that wasn't enough for Oz. He wanted to be a TV star. With a boost from Oprah, that's what he became, and before you could say ka-ching, he was hawking "miracle" weight loss drugs. There was green coffee extract: "You may think magic is make-believe, but this little bean has scientists saying they've found the magic weight-loss cure for every body type." And raspberry ketones. "the No. 1 miracle in a bottle to burn your fat."

He also touted umckaloabo root extract as a cure for cold symptoms (it doesn't work) and lavender soap for leg cramps (don't bother). A 2014 study by Canadian researchers found that only 46% of the advice dispensed on "The Dr. Oz Show" was based on science. The following year, 1,000 physicians signed a letter calling upon Oz to resign from the Columbia faculty. "He's a quack and a fake and a charlatan," wrote Dr. Henry Miller of Stanford.

Maybe prostituting your professional credibility for fraudulent products is nothing to get too exercised about. It certainly isn't new—though the snake oil peddled in the 19th century was at least laced with cocaine or sometimes heroin. But Oz did more than abuse the trust of his audience by selling trash; he veered into outright harm when COVID-19 arrived, advising viewers about a "self-reported" hydroxychloroquine study that showed great results. The con man didn't bother to add that the study had not been peer-reviewed and its subjects consisted only of patients who were already near death.

Dr. Oz abuses every privilege life has handed him. He preys upon people with less knowledge and sophistication. He misleads even when it can cause harm. So, naturally, Sean Hannity is ready to help launch his political career.

Pennsylvania Republicans might have been better off with Parnell, who at least delivers his blows directly, without the smarmy deception.

Cassidy Hutchinson Is a Heroine

July 1, 2022

The House Jan. 6 Committee reportedly decided to rush Cassidy Hutchinson's public testimony out of concern for her personal safety. They have good reason to worry. Consider what Brad Raffensperger, Rusty Bowers, Shaye Moss, Ruby Freeman and too many others to list have been subjected to. Rusty Bowers became a virtual prisoner in his home as his daughter lay dying.

Among the last things Bowers' daughter saw in this life was Trump crowds accusing her father of pedophilia—because he would not betray his oath by lying. Brad Raffensperger's family received specific threats like, "You and your family will be killed very slowly."

Ruby Freeman used to delight in wearing a T-shirt emblazoned with her nickname, "Lady Ruby," but she doesn't dare to wear it now. "I won't even introduce myself by my name anymore." She is afraid every day. "Do you know how it feels to have the president of the United States target you?" Freeman asked. Those words must have been reverberating in Hutchinson's ears as she contemplated her own path.

When Trump first crashed into American politics in 2015, it required only political courage to oppose him. Yet one after another, the leading figures of the GOP, from Chris Christie to Jeff Sessions to Ted Cruz, snapped like dry twigs under his boots.

By 2020, it required more than political courage to stand up to Trump; it required physical courage. Rep. Adam Kinzinger has received death threats not just against himself, but against his wife and 5-month-old baby. Rep. Tom Rice, who voted in favor of Trump's second impeachment, received so many death threats that his chief of staff took to sending some directly to the police and reserving others for the congressman's perusal. (Rice recently lost his primary to a Trump loyalist). So many election workers have been threatened by Trump goons (850, according to Reuters) that three states are considering legislation to protect them.

This is the world that every Republican and conservative brought us by failing to show the minimal amount of integrity. Now they are shamed by the shining example of a 26-year old woman with her life ahead of her, with no motive but love of country and no power except that which comes from a clear conscience.

There has been some tussling over a couple of details of Hutchinson's testimony. Two Secret Service officers reportedly claim that they want to contradict her SUV story under oath. We'll see. Anyone who viewed the presidential debate in 2020 cannot be shocked that Trump can be unhinged. Eric Herschmann says that a note Hutchinson testified to writing was actually written by him. Those are trivial matters compared with what is unrebutted.

It was clear before June 28 that Trump lifted not a finger to end the violence at the Capitol for many hours. Any normal, nonevil person, confronted with the fact that a mob of his supporters was committing violence at the Capitol, would have called them off. Trump did the opposite. He poured gasoline on the fire, tweeting that "Mike Pence didn't have the courage to do what should have been done to protect our Country and our Constitution."

Now we learn from Hutchinson that when some of the nonzombified staff at the White House attempted to get Trump to do the most elementally decent act imaginable—to protect another human being, his own vice president—Trump said, "Mike Pence deserves it." Is it conceivable that Trump could have been so depraved? Yes. Months later, speaking to Jonathan Karl, Trump was asked about his supporters' chants of "Hang Mike Pence." He defended them. "Well, the people were very angry. Because … it's common sense, that you're supposed to protect—How can you, if you know a vote is fraudulent, right—how can you pass on a fraudulent vote to Congress?"

And that, in turn, is consistent with Trump's comment on Jan. 6 when a panicked Kevin McCarthy phoned to beg the president to call off his mob: "Well, Kevin, I guess these people are more upset about the election than you are." Even in the past few months, Trump has been promising to pardon the rioters, should he be reelected. "We love you," he said on Jan. 6. He still does.

So it sure looks like Cassidy Hutchinson is describing the guy we know—the man who was fine with seeing his vice president murdered.

The most frightening thing we've learned over the past six years is just how indifferent the vast majority of the Republican Party is to the rule of law, the Constitution, basic decency and truth. But there have also been ordinary men and women who met the moment with grace and integrity. Their examples prove that the flame of liberty has not been extinguished. If this republic survives, Rep. Liz Cheney will be remembered as a heroine who ensured that it could. And Cassidy Hutchinson will deserve a place of honor for showing a party of cowards what courage looks like.

Mike Pence Sold His Soul for Nothing

July 29, 2022

Mike Pence thinks he has a shot at the presidency.

You can imagine how the conversation went with his political advisors: *People are tired of Trump. They want to move on. And you're the perfect person to fill the void. You served him faithfully, but when it came to violating the Constitution, you stood your ground. And you are the true conservative!*

Marc Short, Pence's vice-presidential chief of staff, offered that, "If he were to run, he may not be the biggest celebrity. But if we're going to go back to a principled conservative who represents the things we stand for, then there's no one better than Mike."

"If we're going to go back." Not likely. But Pence seems to think there's a yearning for that. He's blown the dust off yellowing copies of his Before Time speeches and sprinkled his text with the sort of Christian-y talk that got him a House seat and the Indiana governor's chair: "Pray for our opponents," he told a (small) audience at a South Carolina church.

Isn't that nice? But there are a few flies in the ointment.

First problem. Now? Now is the moment that Pence rolls out the prayer? As Pence is well-situated to know, big chunks of the GOP base have become hungry for a very different tone. Christian charity is out. Vulgar insults, shameless lies and secessionist hatred are in. It sure is ugly, but Pence is in no position to complain. It's a revolution that Pence did so much to encourage, and it's bizarre that he seems to think he can carry on as if nothing has changed.

Pence prostituted his reputation for Christian piety to the most vile figure in the history of American presidential politics, a man who modeled the opposite of every virtue taught in Sunday school. Pence's pious conscience was remarkably quiescent when Trump encouraged his followers to rough up hecklers; when he bore false witness against Muslim Americans (falsely claiming that he saw them celebrating after 9/11); when he attempted to extort the president of Ukraine to lie about Joe Biden; when he separated asylum-seeking parents from their children; when he refused to condemn the tiki-torch Nazi wannabees in Charlottesville; when he elevated a series of kooks and conspiracists to high office; and when he insisted that the election had been stolen.

Pence was fine with all of it.

Second problem: Worse than simply remaining silent, he played the toady with seemingly endless reserves of self-mortification, uttering cringeworthy encomia to Trump's "broad-shouldered leadership" (a phrase he repeated at least 17 times) and audacious lies about matters big and small.

Pence helped transform the GOP from a conservative party into a cult, and as he is discovering to his sorrow, cults don't behave the way normal political parties do. That's why Pence's gamble that he will get credit from the base for his loyal service to the leader is foolhardy. He is at the mercy of the leader. If the leader disowns him, no history of loyalty to Trump himself, far less service to conservative goals, will save him. Ask Jeff Sessions. Ask Mo Brooks.

Third problem: It's impossible to say how large a contingent of Republican primary voters are in the "Pence is a Traitor" camp, but consider that a recent New York Times/Siena poll found that only 6% of Republicans would vote for Pence in a 2024 primary. At their dueling campaign appearances in Arizona, Trump assembled a rally attended by thousands while Pence spoke to a crowd estimated at 300.

There may indeed be an audience in the GOP for someone other than Trump. A softening in his support is now just barely discernible in polling and lack of donor enthusiasm. But the Trump base will not forgive Pence. Better to turn to someone like

Ron DeSantis, who hasn't been guilty of abiding by the Constitution.

And if the GOP were, by some miracle, to seek an honest, non-authoritarian, traditionally conservative candidate, there are other choices including Liz Cheney, Larry Hogan and Adam Kinzinger, who have reminded Republicans of what conservatism can look like.

Pence's tragedy is that he has managed to earn the contempt of the MAGA world and the anti-MAGA world. He deserves full credit for not obeying Trump's command to refuse to count the Electoral College votes on Jan. 6, 2021. But considering the stakes, he should have followed it up with total honesty about how we reached that frightening moment in American democracy. If he had attempted to invoke the 25th Amendment, or encouraged senators to convict Trump at the second impeachment, or testified in public to the House Jan. 6 Committee, it might have gone some way to compensate for the infamy of the past four years.

Pence chose another path—trying to have it both ways. It will end, perhaps appropriately, with a whimper.

The GOP Can't Whatabout the Pelosi Attack

Nov. 4, 2022

The House speaker's husband was brutally attacked, and most GOP officeholders—even the "good Republicans" we've been assured will usher us out of Trumpism—failed the test.

A handful still had enough of a decency default to find the right words. Mitch McConnell tweeted his concern, as did Mike Pence. But the former president was silent. Most elected Republicans were as well.

Kevin McCarthy took his time. He didn't tweet for most of the day except to say, through an aide, that he had reached out privately to Nancy Pelosi. That's nice, but that's not what the situation calls for. The crucial thing is to condemn the act publicly and leave no doubt that when it comes to acts of violence and terrorism, there are no Democrats or Republicans, only Americans. On Saturday evening, Kevin McCarthy finally found it within himself to say the attack was "wrong" but immediately vitiated the sentiment with heavy-handed whataboutism. "We've watched this with Lee Zeldin, we've watched this with Supreme Court justices, this is wrong—violence should not go. You watch what happened to Steve Scalise and others. This has got to stop." McCarthy's list contained only Republican victims.

While Paul Pelosi was in surgery, Gov. Glenn Youngkin told a campaign crowd that "Speaker Pelosi's husband, they had a break-in last night in their house, and he was assaulted. There's no room for violence anywhere, but we're gonna send her back to be with him in California. That's what we're going to go do." Very tasteful. The audience naturally cheered, because crowds, especially at political rallies, are not given to sober reflection.

That's why leaders must set the right tone.

So even the "normal" Republicans are, if not trolls themselves, troll adjacent.

Chris Sununu, another Republican who seemed, if you squinted just the right way, to be normal, appeared on "Meet the Press" the day after Pelosi was attacked. Sununu looked wise when he declined to run for the Senate and accurately characterized Don Bolduc, the GOP's eventual Senate candidate, as "not serious, a conspiracy type" back in the spring. Today though, Sununu is supporting Bolduc because he wears the correct jersey. So it's not terribly surprising that he lapsed into whataboutism, saying that "This started back in the summer of 2020, right, when you saw cities burning, you saw not a whole lot of accountability there."

This is a version of a Republican talking point. Democrats failed to condemn the violence that followed the murder of George Floyd, they say, so they have unclean hands when it comes to the violence committed by Trump's mob on Jan. 6. While it's true that some Democrats seemed soft on antifa violence in the summer of 2020, there are a few flaws with the argument. For one thing, leading Democrats, including the party's presidential nominee, did condemn the violence repeatedly. Second, the rioters were not acting as agents of any political party. They were not called into the streets by the president of the United States with the words "stand by" and "will be wild!" They were not carrying flags emblazoned with Biden's name. And third, while the violence that followed Floyd's murder was unconscionable and extremely destructive of property, it was not political except in a very abstract sense. It was not designed to, and could not have, affected the outcome of any election, for example. Nor did it involve threats of violence against political figures. There was tremendous property damage, but no gallows erected for Republican officeholders and no rioters chanting, "Hang Donald Trump."

Democrats have not fetishized guns and violence as the GOP has. They have not elevated to hero status a young man, Kyle

Rittenhouse, who shot his way into a protest, killing a man; nor featured gun brandishing suburbanites at their national convention; nor filled their commercials and even their Christmas cards with images of themselves bedecked with weaponry.

So Sununu's bothsidesism breaks down.

Nor is there anything to compete with the GOP's descent into sheer brutishness. Remember Larry Elder, noting that Paul Pelosi had been arrested for a DUI a few months ago, tweeted: "Poor Paul Pelosi. First, he's busted for DUI and then gets attacked in his home. Hammered twice in six months."

What the hell is wrong with these people?

All of this is a garden party compared with the bilge (thank you, Charlie Sykes) released into the atmosphere by Donald Trump Jr. Repeating a rumor from the fever swamps (which rumor was later retweeted by the new chief Twit), he displayed a picture of men's underwear and a hammer, saying "Got my Paul Pelosi Halloween costume ready." The vile, baseless claim that Pelosi was in the midst of a homosexual tryst with his attacker thus became the official conservative response to a horrifying attack on a defenseless 82-year-old man.

It's beginning to look like Republicans go along with Trumpism not because they feel they must, but because they've really come to embody it.

It Couldn't Happen to a Nicer Guy

Jan. 6, 2023

Here's a funny thing about the Freedom Caucus' insurrection against Kevin McCarthy, which on Tuesday denied him election as Speaker of the House on three consecutive ballots for the first time in a century. On the surface, it looks like the firebrands and zealots are in revolt against the GOP "establishment." But the reality is that the Republican establishment is deader than dead. It's hard to date its demise with precision, but Jan. 6, 2021, is a good marker. That was a second date that should live in infamy—a date when, following a violent assault on the Capitol, two-thirds of the Republican caucus voted with the mob. The battle unfolding over the speakership is not between the extremists and the establishment. It's between two camps of extremists.

McCarthy, like all of the members of the Freedom Caucus who are attempting to thwart him, refused to certify Joe Biden's victory in the Electoral College. Like the Freedom Caucus, McCarthy has faithfully repeated the lie about the 2020 election being stolen. Like them, he has fanned the flames of conspiracism, pushed for an end to the military's COVID-19 vaccine mandate, helped Harriet Hageman defeat Liz Cheney in the Wyoming primary and enfolded Marjorie Taylor Greene in a great bear hug. He's game for impeaching Alejandro Mayorkas, investigating Hunter Biden's laptop and removing the magnetometers at the entrance to the House floor. McCarthy has been indistinguishable from House Freedom Caucus members when it comes to matters of civic virtue, too. He failed to condemn the brutal attack on Paul Pelosi, contenting himself with a private note to Speaker Pelosi, and was silent after Trump dined with Kanye West and Nick Fuentes. He has threatened to remove

Eric Swalwell, Ilhan Omar and Adam Schiff from their committees as revenge for Greene's treatment by Democrats. He has expressed skepticism about aid to Ukraine, vowing that there would be no "blank check." What more could the Freedom Caucus demand?

In fact, as the clock ticked down to the vote for speaker, McCarthy was willing to give in to every demand of the Freedom Caucus, even including the "motion to vacate the chair," which would permit five members of Congress to call a vote for the speaker's removal whenever they chose.

If there were an establishment GOP remaining, it would recoil from the positions staked out by the leadership of the Freedom Caucus. Rep. Andy Biggs, who led the caucus from 2019 to 2022, refused to wear a mask even at the height of the pandemic. He sought a presidential pardon for his role in the fake elector scheme. He voted against giving medals to the Capitol police who behaved heroically on Jan. 6. He opposed aid to Ukraine on the grounds that the border with Mexico remains unsecured. And he voted against admitting Sweden and Finland to NATO.

Bigg's successor as Freedom Caucus chair is Scott Perry, who voted against a House resolution condemning the QAnon conspiracy, endorsed the "great replacement" garbage and played a major role in the attempted coup of Jan. 6. His texts to Mark Meadows reveal not a conservative but a borderline nut. He forwarded links to YouTube videos suggesting that votes had been manipulated by Italian satellites and recommended that Jeffrey Clark, a fellow refugee from reality, be installed as attorney general. Like Biggs, he requested a presidential pardon.

These views do not place the Freedom Caucus on the right. They simply place them outside the realm of reason. And yet McCarthy, the supposed avatar of the Republican establishment, has been willing to surrender to their demands. His flexibility has not been rewarded only because they don't really have demands. They don't care about policy. If they did, they would seek something in exchange for their support. They haven't. There is no price McCarthy would not stoop to pay—but they don't have concrete goals other than posturing as anti-establishment. There is no way for McCarthy to negotiate with people whose only aim is to be seen as opposing him.

It's the logical end point of a party that has descended into mindless demonization—of Democrats, of immigrants, of the "deep state," of the FBI, of the medical profession, of the "woke" military—and now of one another. It's hard to see how they can be trusted with power.

Chapter Two: The Rise of Trumpism

The Challenge for Republicans

Nov. 9, 2016

My feelings this morning are so radically mixed that my brain resembles a Cuisinart. I cannot help but be glad that Hillary Clinton was defeated. I am shaking my head in amazement about the Senate, and accordingly about the Supreme Court.

The election results feel like a gorgeous, gleaming new BMW in the driveway. But instead of a bow on the roof, there's a vial of nitroglycerin.

I wish president-elect Donald Trump nothing but good this morning. I pray for him and for the country, but fingers of fear still grip my heart. The glow of victory cannot obscure or perfume who the man is. Trump has demonstrated emotional unsteadiness, cruelty, and wild irresponsibility. He is most unhinged when his fragile ego is wounded. He is, in many ways, a spoiled child.

His character is the great challenge for the nation and the Republican Party going forward. On this post-election morning, it seems advisable that those Republicans who signed statements of opposition to him—particularly foreign policy experts—reassess. A president has the most scope for independent action on the world stage, and it is there that he can do the maximum amount of damage. Trump has indulged in ignorant bluster to gain popularity (he would crush ISIS "very quickly," "take the oil" from the Middle East, renegotiate NAFTA, force Mexico to pay for a border wall, "get along very well" with Vladimir Putin, and encourage nuclear proliferation). But one thing we know about Trump is that he will say almost anything for attention and effect, and he has contradicted himself thousands of times. He will need advisers with experience, judgment, and keen psychological skills to temper his instincts and guide him toward policies more in line with American interests and values. Even foreign policy experts who were appalled by Trump's campaign rhetoric—in fact, especially they—should consider serving in his administration.

Trump has been on both sides of most of the contentious issues in American life. He's been pro and anti socialized medicine, for and against (mostly) entitlement reform, for (mostly) and against abortion. He is, primarily, an entertainer, who hasn't given much thought to public policy at all, but is expert at playing to a crowd and ventilating its resentments. But even more than riling up his audiences, Trump's lodestar has always been himself. Everything comes back to him, especially when he's feeling attacked or disrespected.

I am praying that because he will now have his heart's desire—the nonstop shower of attention and yes, flattery, that comes with the Oval Office, that this will serve as a tonic for his outsized ego and perhaps supply him the calm he will need to serve wisely.

Others will need wisdom as well. After the shock of his victory wears off, the press will return to treating him as radioactive—which will be taken by his supporters and much of the Republican Party as evidence that he must be right. That's a mistake for both sides. The mainstream press is biased, openly so, and they need to swallow hard and own it. That doesn't mean they are always wrong. As I've said often during the general election, the press and Democrats have cried wolf on racism and xenophobia so many times that they've discredited themselves. A few (Bill Maher, for example) have acknowledged as much. But what the Republican grass roots did not grapple with adequately is that this time, many of the outrageous charges the media trotted out were true. Their job was easy. All they had to do was quote the candidate, not dig through his middle school records to find some prank. Trump has said reprehensible things and winked at open bigotry. He is indecent and loutish. The right-wing media Trump empowered have circulated absurd conspiracies and lies. They are no better, and in some ways they are worse, than the "lying media" they despise. Our duty to stand for responsible journalism and to rebuke the Brietbarts and InfoWars types only grows more urgent this morning.

Trump has frightening, undemocratic impulses. He admires strongmen. But—perhaps this is a saving grace—he also has a notoriously short attention span. The great challenge for Republicans will be to oppose him if (when?) he strays in dangerous directions as president, whether in restricting civil liberties, undermining international alliances, inaugurating devastating trade wars, or casting aside constitutional restraints on executive power. This will be the most difficult of trials for Republican officeholders, because their constituents will not thank them for it, only their posterity.

May God grant all the charity and grace to navigate the uncharted waters we're in.

Patriotism, Not Nationalism

Feb. 17, 2017

National Review has sparked an important debate about nationalism. As someone who has been accused throughout her life of excessive love of country (can't count the number of times I've been reproached for arguing that despite slavery, Jim Crow and the internment of JapaneseAmericans, our country is eminently lovable), I feel a bit awkward rebutting anything that travels under the name "Love of Country." Nevertheless, I must join Jonah Goldberg, Yuval Levin, Ben Shapiro and others in demurring from Rich Lowry and Ramesh Ponnuru's defense of nationalism.

Lowry and Ponnuru are two of the writers I most admire (at a time when that group is shrinking fast). If they make an argument with which I disagree, I'm inclined to question my own judgment. So I remain open to the possibility that they are right. But it seems to me that their willingness to believe that nationalism, as opposed to patriotism, can be benign is not convincing.

Everything they assert about the naturalness of nationalism—it arises out of the same soil as love of family, community, church, etc.—is true of patriotism. It's true, as Lowry and Ponnuru note, that the left has discredited itself over the years by its hostility to sincere patriotism.

Patriotism is enough—it needs no improving or expanding.

Nationalism is something else. It's hard to think of a nationalist who does not pervert patriotism into something aggressive—against foreign adversaries, domestic minorities or both. When Mexican President Lazaro Cardenas nationalized the oil industry in 1938 (expropriating the property of hated foreigners), he was favored with a chanting crowd of 100,000 supporters in Mexico City. Gamal Abdel Nasser's nationalism found expression in nationalization (of the Suez Canal in that case) and also in aggressive war against Israel and Yemen. Vladimir Putin's nationalism has been characterized by demonization of the United States in domestic propaganda and his invasion of neighboring countries. Benito Mussolini believed in reclaiming Italy's lost glory and invaded Abyssinia (Ethiopia) to fulfill his vision.

Our own history is not pristine. We've had our moments of belligerent nationalism. The Mexican-American War, for example, was a pure land grab. Lowry and Ponnuru cite President Lincoln as an example of a benign nationalist, but he recognized corrupt nationalism in his own time. As a member of Congress, he deplored the Mexican-American War in the strongest terms, accusing President Polk of misleading the public about on whose territory hostilities began, and thundering, "The blood of this war, like the blood of Abel, is crying to Heaven." I'm not proposing that we return California to the Mexicans (though, considering their voting patterns, it's tempting), but the war that brought California (and other states) into our union was not our finest hour. It was, arguably, the hour of maximal American nationalism.

I believe that nationalism is a demagogue's patriotism. Demagogues of the right and left both play upon natural and even benevolent instincts for their own purposes. The left's demagogues distort love of justice and equality into a leveling desire to scapegoat others. Bernie Sanders doesn't just appeal to people's desire for fairness; he encourages them to believe that they are the victims of the "1%," who are siphoning all of the nation's wealth for themselves. If you are poor, Sanders claims, it is because someone who is rich has taken your share.

Demagogues of the right—or nationalists—argue that our troubles are the result of immigrants taking our jobs or foreigners stealing our factories. This is not natural love of home and hearth or reverence for America's founding ideals. It is scapegoating.

Which brings us to the proximate cause of this debate:

President Trump. Far from deepening our appreciation of our history or institutions, he embodies the reasons to be wary of demagoguery in the name of country. In him we see strutting nationalism ("America first!") but little true patriotism. He claims to pursue America's interests, yet has shockingly little respect for the nation he heads. He doesn't love the country enough to have familiarized himself with the basics of our system. In one debate, he said judges "sign bills," and in a Capitol Hill meeting with congressmen, he praised Article XII of the Constitution. What patriot can claim that we lack the moral authority to criticize Turkey's crackdown on independent journalists, or impugn this country as no better than Russia when it comes to political assassination? As Trump demonstrates, nationalism is not patriotism in a hurry; it is resentment draped in the flag.

In his concurrence with Lowry/Ponnuru, John O'Sullivan indirectly makes a similar point, defending Trump's disavowal of American exceptionalism. O'Sullivan offers that this is delicacy on Trump's part. "He doesn't want to humiliate the foreigners who will shortly be losing to America. ... When you intend to shoot a man, it costs nothing to be polite."

That's not my idea of patriotism.

Anger Games

May 19, 2017

"Hate is a more powerful motivator than love." According to the new Netflix documentary "Get Me Roger Stone," that is one of the "rules" the self-described Republican "agent provocateur" has lived by. Stone, of course, is a showman. The "evil political operator" pose is to some degree an artifice—a brand he's selling. Still, his style of politics has now moved from the wings to center stage. We're engaged in an experiment to see how much damage we can do to our society by adopting Stone's rules.

The new Stone documentary (clearly produced by left-leaning filmmakers) forms a precise bookend to the 2016 documentary "Weiner" that followed former Democratic congressman Anthony Weiner throughout his pyrotechnic downfall. Weiner's bid for the mayoralty of New York City—for those lucky enough to have forgotten the details—was derailed by revelations that he had not put his addiction to sexting with strangers behind him. To watch the cringe-inducing Anthony Weiner (estranged husband of Hillary Clinton's "body man" Huma Abedin) permit cameras to record not just mortifying encounters with his wife but also the candidate spinning lies for public consumption is to see the peculiarly 21st century disease of narcissism at a high water mark. Not even when the most humiliating details of his behavior were being ogled by the whole world did Weiner consider telling the trailing documentarians to turn off the cameras.

The Weiner saga bubbled back to the surface, like a herpes outbreak, in October 2016, when the FBI found that Huma Abedin had apparently forwarded emails to Weiner's laptop, thus potentially passing national secrets to an unsecure device, and

James Comey announced that the investigation into the Clinton emails was back on.

Stone is the Republican yin to Weiner's yang. He proffers bits of philosophy such as "It's better to be infamous than never to be famous at all." He achieved his infamy the way Weiner did—with a flamboyant sex scandal, when he was working on the Dole presidential campaign in 1996. Those were the days, children, when being a "swinger" was enough to discredit a Republican, and Stone was banished.

He returned, trailing sulfur as cologne, with the candidacy of Donald Trump. Stone apparently encouraged Trump to push the "birther" conspiracy. He gleefully initiated chants of "Lock her up!" at Trump rallies, threw an encouraging arm around the shoulders of InfoWars conspiracy peddler Alex Jones, called Julian Assange a "hero" and overtly warned Republican delegates who might consider voting for another candidate at the Republican Convention in Cleveland that his operatives had their "hotel room numbers."

Stone was separated from the Trump campaign at some point, though he claims to have continuing contact with the president, and he certainly set a tone.

So this is the world we inhabit now—where pathological narcissism goes either unrecognized or at least unpunished. Stone and Weiner were not ejected from the national bloodstream. Both were/are incredibly close to the leaders of our parties. How is that possible for a healthy republic?

It isn't. We're not healthy right now. We are in a state of perpetual partisan rage; a fever stoked by interests who are making money from the clown-show ratings. CNN and MSNBC do wall-to-wall outrage, 24/7, about each and every Trump misstep (and they come thick and fast)—keeping the needle more or less permanently dialed to 11. They perpetually label Trump a "conservative" only because they despise Trump and they loathe conservatives and assume that the two must be coterminous.

Fox News has become, with a few rare exceptions, the Trump Ministry of Information—minimizing every mistake, justifying every outrage as a legitimate response to the "media frenzy" against him, and highlighting every hot-button news story that can enrage/frighten viewers about campus authoritarians, illegal immigrants, terrorists and Democrats.

The Trump presidency could only be possible in a country that makes few distinctions between fame and notoriety, and that has been rubbed raw by ceaseless incitement. Throughout his career, Trump did one thing extraordinarily well—keep himself the center of attention. His talent for controversy and "trolling" kept him successful and famous. "He fights," people noted admiringly. Yes, but only for himself. As we're seeing, now that serious blunders are becoming an almost daily affair, incessant belligerence is exhausting for everyone and self-sabotaging for Trump. It turns out that swinging a mace in all directions is not "just what Washington, D.C., needed," far less the country.

But the ratings are great.

Contra Fox News, Trump Is the Threat to Civilization

June 26, 2020

This election "is no longer about Donald Trump's tweeting," conservative historian Victor Davis Hanson told Fox News host Tucker Carlson the other night. Nor is it about "a lockdown, the virus, the economy (or) foreign policy. It's an existential question … and I'm going to vote for civilization."

Ah, the conservative warning of barbarians at the gate. It's a hardy perennial. I recognize it because, as a conservative myself, I'm in sympathy with it—to a point. In "The Righteous Mind," Jonathan Haidt observed that both progressives and conservatives are motivated by morality, but their hierarchies are different. Progressives tend to value care, especially for victims of oppression, while conservatives cherish order and sanctity. Conservatives are hypersensitive to threats to order. This is neither good nor bad, it's just a fact. Order is no small virtue in a polity and progressives shouldn't discount it. Arguably, it's the foundation for other virtues progressives treasure such as fairness.

The conservative battle cry in response to the dreadful news of the past three months is to point to the mobs toppling statues as evidence that safety and security are threatened (just as they claimed in 2018 that the caravan from Central America would upend American civilization). Sean Hannity warns that if Donald Trump is defeated, then "America will become unrecognizable." Laura Ingraham described the Democratic agenda as hoping "to pull down our whole culture: the American founding, western civilization and everything that sprang from it."

Mobs are never attractive, whether in the streets or on cable opinion shows, and they are not exactly discriminating in their iconoclasm. In addition to statues of Confederate generals and slave traders, other monuments targeted have included those of Hans Christian Heg, an abolitionist who died fighting for the Union at the battle of Chickamauga in 1863, and Ulysses Grant, who defeated the Confederacy.

Disorder in the streets is an engraved invitation to a right-wing backlash. But there are two reasons that the current conservative appeal to law and order is several tones flat. The first is that while there has been some rioting and looting, the vast majority of protests have been peaceful and the trajectory is toward less, not more, violence. The second problem with the call to defend the gates of civilization is this: Donald Trump is the barbarian.

An orderly society is not one that performatively hugs the American flag but one that upholds the rule of law for which it stands. Throughout his administration, Trump has demonstrated contempt for law. He has violated campaign finance laws by paying off a porn star, flouted legal subpoenas from Congress and other duly constituted authorities looking into administration actions, abused Article II power by dangling pardons to former associates facing criminal trials, unlawfully diverted Defense Department funds to begin building a border wall, wrongly fired numerous inspectors general and encouraged police to rough up arrestees—among uncountable other violations. He has attempted to strong-arm an ally to invent lies about his domestic opposition and begged for other foreign leaders to help his election prospects. His attorney general is diligently attempting to reward his friends and punish his (perceived) enemies—exactly what happens in corrupt dictatorships.

In addition to respect for the law, a thriving civilization requires a certain minimum level of integrity and honor in its people, particularly in its leaders. This president is not just the most dishonest person ever to darken 1600 Pennsylvania Ave., he and his enablers have made war on the very concept of truth. They do this not just by lying but by lying *when there are videotapes*.

They demand that, knowing the truth, you assent to their lies as obeisance to power.

The annihilation of truth permits the cultivation of group hatreds. Trump's followers are led to despise supposedly criminal immigrants, "disloyal" Republicans, ungrateful allies, the press, the courts and the "deep state." Election results are to be distrusted—and elections are to be thwarted where they cannot be fairly won. Any unflattering portrayal is "fake news." Conspiracy theories that any competent fifth grader can detect as bogus grace the president's Twitter feed.

One of the most admirable features of our civilization is our dedication to human dignity. While imperfectly implemented, our basic commitment to human rights around the globe has been an aspiration shared by Democrats and Republicans. But with a barbarian in the Oval Office, we are now "falling in love" with Kim Jong Un, praising Rodrigo Duterte for extrajudicial murders, defending Vladimir Putin by suggesting that we are just as guilty of murdering our enemies as he and giving the green light to China to build concentration camps for a million innocent Uighurs.

So a statue or two may unjustly bite the dust, but the greater threat to law and order and yes, civilization, is the guy at the Resolute Desk.

Don't Let Trump Discredit Patriotism

Oct. 22, 2020

Donald Trump has a documented history of driving Americans away from the policies he favors. This is both good and bad.

As Catherine Rampell noted, the president has moved American public opinion toward greater approval of immigration. The percentage of Americans who said that immigration is good for the country bounced around in the 50s and 60s in the first decade and a half of this century. But since 2016, the trend has been up sharply. In 2020, 77% of Americans told Gallup that they think immigration is good for the country. Similarly, the percentage who believe that accepting refugees fleeing war or persecution should be a priority has increased from 62% in 2016 to 73% in 2019.

Trump has also increased the appetite for government involvement in health care. Since embarking on his quest for the presidency, Trump has denounced the Affordable Care Act, but only because he promised something superior. His specific policy proposal for replacing the law was something "terrific," "phenomenal" and "fantastic." In February 2017, having been in office a few weeks, Trump tweeted "repeal and replacement of ObamaCare is coming fast!" At the end of March, with negotiations bogging down, he pleaded for more time. "I want to have a great health care bill and plan, and we will."

It didn't happen. Health care reform was a dead letter, except that having failed to repeal or replace the ACA through legislation, the administration joined in a legal assault on the law, challenging its constitutionality. If the Trump administration were to get its way at the Supreme Court, millions of Americans would lose health insurance in the midst of a pandemic. Oh, and on Aug. 3 of this year, the president once again promised his own health care proposal "hopefully, prior to the end of the month."

Amazingly, the public's response to this clown show was to express increasing support for the ACA, with a solid 55% expressing approval of the law this month, up from about 40% in 2016.

Trump's fulminations against trade have convinced some—Republicans are now far more negative about NAFTA than in the pre-Trump era—but most Americans have moved in the other direction, with 74% agreeing that trade is an opportunity for economic growth versus 21% who view it as a threat to the economy.

As a pro-immigrant free-trader, I'm not sorry that Trump has driven people away from his views, though I do lament the loss of a chance for free market health reform.

Trump has driven people away from the Republican Party, and caused them to reject the label "conservative." And while it's no loss for the nation if protectionism and nativism are discredited, there are other things that Trumpism endangers that would be serious losses.

I worry that Trump is contaminating patriotism itself. His blatantly racist appeals combined with his crude and offensive invocations of "America First" run the risk of associating patriotism with whiteness. His fondness for the Confederacy stains his embrace of the American flag.

What Trump's fans on the right never seem to grapple with as they ceaselessly invoke the specter of socialism, riots and gun confiscation, is how much Trump drives the left toward extremism. From the 1619 Project to the toppling of statues of anti-slavery heroes, there is a movement afoot that Bari Weiss calls a "mixture of postmodernism, postcolonialism, identity politics, neo-Marxism, critical race theory, intersectionality, and the therapeutic mentality." Some of this predated Trump, of course, but he has turbo-charged it.

The left-wing challenge to American legitimacy has always

stressed racism, colonialism, sexism and unconstrained capitalism. Trump has lived down to each and every one of those stereotypes. (You may object that he wasn't a colonialist, but don't forget, "Take the oil!")

As we look to rebuild in a post-Trump world, we non-leftists must be able to make the case for American patriotism. We cannot respond to the 1619 Project with heavy-handed attempts to limit its reach, but with arguments and context. No, this country would not be lovable if its history were one long chronicle of racism and oppression. It isn't. We have much to be ashamed of in our history but much more to celebrate and be grateful for. We have been free and a beacon of freedom for more than two centuries. We have welcomed people from all over the globe and insisted that when they become citizens, they are the full equals of those born here. We have confronted our past sins, imperfectly, but diligently, nevertheless. We've given the world fantastic inventions like the airplane and the Salk vaccine, but nothing more important than the Declaration of Independence with its ringing invocation of natural rights.

Trump is a shriveled soul and tends to diminish everything and everyone he touches. As we move out of his orbit, we can begin to recapture some of the grandeur of the nation he has led so miserably.

We cannot permit American patriotism to be hijacked by yahoos and bigots. As we start to heal from the past four years, we must rescue patriotism from Trumpism.

Trump's First Victim—Truth

Dec. 4, 2020

The photo looks faked. It's so heavy-handed. A grinning Australian soldier, his insignia clear as day on his helmet and arm, stands on the Australian flag holding a small, barefoot Afghan child in front of him. He grasps a bloody knife to the child's throat. The caption reads "Don't be afraid, we are coming to bring you peace!"

This not particularly well-disguised piece of propaganda (it's the work of Chinese graphic artist Fu Yu, aka Qilin) was posted to Twitter by the government of China, part of a broad-based campaign China is waging against Australia. Why? Simple: Australia has told the truth.

Marise Payne, Australia's foreign minister, delivered a scathing speech to the U.N. Human Rights Council in September outlining China's many human rights abuses, including the maltreatment of Uighurs and the repressive measures China has lately adopted toward Hong Kong. This has infuriated Beijing, which has retaliated by imposing sanctions against a lengthening list of Australian products, and now, a disinformation attack.

The ammunition was supplied, indirectly, by Australia itself. Like other free countries, Australia investigates itself, and a recent report found that Australian soldiers had killed 39 Afghan civilians. Upon the report's release, Angus Campbell, chief of the defense forces, apologized to the Afghan people and to the Australian people, and the Australian government is looking into paying compensation to the families of those wrongly killed.

China took the nugget of truth—Australian forces had committed war crimes—and transformed it into a ghoulish image of a rapacious Aussie about to sacrifice an innocent child.

I said at the start that the photo looks faked—who poses for war crimes pictures on a flag tableau? And yet, in our time, truth has become more elusive than ever. Technology presents real challenges. How many people in China and around the world will view that photo and believe it's real? And we keep hearing about the "deep fakes"—doctored video images—that are around the corner. How many would believe a fraudulent video image of say, Hunter Biden confessing to child abuse?

In an era when technology can produce phony images and doctored videos of real people doing and saying things they never did or said, the question of how to find truth becomes ever more urgent.

Credibility comes down to reputation—which is why we have much damage to our own standing to repair.

President Donald Trump's assault on truth and his insistence that all news critical of him is fake is reminiscent of the world's worst regimes. The first thing to go when the jackboots come is the free press. Trump's attacks on the press were rhetorical, not literal. But it's no coincidence that his term, "fake news," has become a favorite of thugs worldwide.

During the Cold War, it was understood that the West, for all its flaws, was more honest than the Communist bloc because of the free press. The media in the old USSR was full of cheerful workers exceeding their quotas and ruddy farmers luxuriating in golden fields of wheat. The late Daniel Patrick Moynihan had a succinct summation of the state of play. "When we travel about the world and come to a country whose newspapers are filled with bad news we feel that liberty lives in that land," he quipped, "When we come to a country whose newspapers are filled with good news, we feel differently."

The governments of free countries, of course, attempt to lie. But at least the free press can often expose them, and fear of exposure keeps them in check to some degree.

Reputation matters. It's why China is so incensed that Australia has had the temerity to criticize it. Why do we trust Canberra more than Beijing? Because the Australians are free and accountable. They've admitted their war crimes and agonized over them. The Chinese have never acknowledged their far more massive human toll. Even without going back to the Great Leap Forward—the most devastating catastrophe in China's history, causing between 18 million and 45 million starvation deaths—we have the Tiananmen massacre within living memory, the rape of Tibet, and, of course, the widespread infanticide accompanying the One Child policy.

Our own reputation for honesty has taken a severe hit under Trump. How will other nations trust the word of the U.S. when we elected someone who supported the lies of Kim Jong Un and other corrupt and cruel dictators, and valorized our own war criminals? What does it tell the world when our president conducts a nonstop jihad against the press? Who can respect this nation when our president expressed his belief, in defending Vladimir Putin, that we commit just as many sins?

Australia is showing courage by standing up to China, and paying a price. The White House has announced this week that it will be serving Australian wine, which would have been a better gesture if this president had not allied us with the world's liars and criminals for four years.

In the post-Trump era, the most important restoration will be that of truth.

Trumpism Triumphant—Even in Defeat

Dec. 9, 2020

Off and on for 25 years, I participated in National Review cruises as a speaker. I met lots of wonderful people who were intelligent, curious and great company—but there were always cranks and conspiracy theorists, too. Once, during the Clinton administration, people at my dinner table were repeating the story that Hillary Clinton had killed Vince Foster. I choked down my bite of chicken Kiev and responded, as equably as possible, "Well, for that to be true, she would also have had to transport his body to Fort Marcy Park without the Secret Service or anyone else noticing." Several people at the table blinked back at me. *Yeah? So?*

In later years, I noticed that cruisers weren't citing mainstream publications for their information. They were getting their news from email lists and subscription newsletters.

There's a theory that people have rallied around President Donald Trump and alternative news sources because they feel disrespected by the mainstream, liberal-leaning press. There is some truth in this, but my experience with conservatives makes me skeptical of that as a complete explanation. Sure, the urban/rural divide is real—and not limited to the United States—but resentment of elites has always been with us. From suspicion of the First Bank of the United States among the Jeffersonians to the populist movement of the 1890s, "coastal elites" have always been despised by some. But it didn't drive people into abject lunacy in the past, or at least not on the scale we see today.

A theme that unified these conspiracy-minded people was a sense of superiority—not inferiority. They felt that they had access to the hidden truth that the deluded masses didn't understand. It was a key feature of Rush Limbaugh's appeal. He has frequently suggested that he understands that ugly reality beneath the polite fictions.

After decades of this diet, and with an enormous turbocharge from Trump, the conspiracists are in the driver's seat of the Republican Party. This is profoundly worrying, because, let's face it: They've suspended their critical faculties. Trump spent months saying mail-in ballots were ripe for fraud. He openly declared that he would not accept the legitimacy of any election he were to lose. He pressured friendly state legislatures, like Pennsylvania's, not to count mailed-in ballots until Election Day so that he could weave a story of victory if he were to do well with in-person voting on election night, knowing that the count for mailed-in ballots would take longer.

Now consider the average Republican voter. If anyone of his or her personal acquaintance were to say about an upcoming company baseball game that the refs are all corrupt and the other team always cheats, and then, after losing the game, claim that it was all rigged, the voter would roll his or her eyes and say, "That guy is a little cracked."

But the normal, ordinary evaluations of character and credibility are suspended in Trump's case.

His legal challenges to the election results have been so absurd that if they'd been filed by anyone other than the president of the United States, they might have been thrown out as "frivolous." They have lost or withdrawn more than 50 suits they've filed—and not just lost but lost with blistering smackdowns from the judges, including those appointed by Trump. "Voters, not lawyers, choose the president," wrote Stephanos Bibas, a judge for the 3rd Circuit Court of Appeals.

In case you missed it, the Republican Party of Arizona is apparently actually asking Republicans to "fight and die" for Trump's stolen-election lie. Retweeting Trumpist Ali Alexander, who said, "I am willing to give my life for this fight," the Arizona GOP replied: "He is. Are you?" (The account has since deleted the tweets.)

Former national security adviser Michael Flynn is calling for a military coup. One of the president's lawyers suggested that an official who oversaw election cybersecurity be shot at dawn.

Even more disturbing than the crackpot statements of hardcore cultists are the Republican elected officials who are behaving like automatons stamped out of a brain removal factory. The Washington Post contacted all of the Republicans serving in the House and Senate to ask who won the election. Two said Trump. Twenty-seven said Joe Biden. And 88% *declined to say*. Ted Cruz, Mr. "Constitutional Conservative," volunteered to argue Trump's utterly fraudulent stolen-election case before the Supreme Court. The court has other ideas.

And then there are the polls showing that shocking numbers of rank-and-file Republicans are buying this big lie. A YouGov/Economist poll found that 73% of Republicans have little or no confidence that the election was conducted fairly. A Morning Consult/Politico survey found that 67% of Republicans say the election was probably or definitely not free and fair. And a Monmouth University poll found 76% of Republicans are "not too confident" or "not at all confident" that the 2020 election was conducted fairly and accurately. Sixty-four Republican members of the Pennsylvania House of Representatives have signed a letter asking members of Congress to throw out Pennsylvania's slate of electors.

We have now reached the stage where it isn't just that Republicans fail to rebuke Trump and are frightened into silence by fear of the base; it's that a critical mass of the Republican Party has adopted Trump's disordered personality for its own. The Republican Party is, in this iteration, a danger to American democracy. Our urgent task is—to borrow a phrase—to repeal and replace it.

Will Trump Face the Music, Finally?

Feb. 18, 2021

There has been some cheering about the 10 House and seven Senate Republicans who voted for impeachment. All honor to those who took the difficult path. But, good God! The president attempted to steal the election. He launched an insurrection against Congress. That only a handful of Republicans could vote to convict him is a sign of deep rot.

It also leaves millions of Americans who thirst for justice unsatisfied. Chances of a criminal indictment for incitement to riot are slim.

What else?

Many are placing hopes in a Fulton County, Georgia, district attorney who is investigating whether Trump's call to Brad Raffensperger demanding that he "find" 11,780 votes was the crime of election fraud. New York's attorney general is investigating Trump's possibly deceptive manipulation of property values to avoid taxes, while the Manhattan district attorney is probing the Trump organizations' "possibly extensive and protracted criminal conduct."

Additionally, Trump could be the target of multiple civil cases arising from the events of Jan. 6. The NAACP has filed suit on behalf of Rep. Bennie Thompson against Trump and Rudy Giuliani alleging that they violated the Reconstruction-era Ku Klux Klan Act by conspiring with white supremacist groups to prevent members of Congress from executing their constitutional duties. The list of possible future plaintiffs includes the families of the seven people who died on Jan. 6 or immediately thereafter, the 138 Capitol and D.C. metropolitan police officers who suffered broken ribs, lost fingers and eyes, and endured concussions, burns, heart attacks and psychological injuries.

Even Mitch McConnell, after voting to acquit Trump on jurisdictional grounds, issued an unconcealed plea for some sort of accountability: "President Trump … didn't get away with anything—yet."

We need some sense that you cannot trample norms and laws with impunity. We need a sense that truth still matters, that justice is not an illusion and that you cannot "get away with" causing the worst subversion of American democracy since the Civil War.

So, godspeed to all the prosecutors, IRS officials, and lawyers who are assembling cases against Trump. Judges and juries are less likely to be conned than millions of voters.

We know in advance what Trumpworld will say about the coming legal tsunami. They will seize upon the favorite dodge of criminal officeholders worldwide—political motivation. They will claim that every suit or indictment is part of the conspiracy against Trump and Trump followers. They will proclaim, as they have about the Mueller investigation, the dozens of women who've accused Trump of abuse and worse, and both impeachments, that they are fatally flawed because they're "politically motivated."

This is the off-the-shelf excuse for every corrupt politician, and Trump's shelf appears to be unusually well stocked. Responding to the Georgia criminal inquiry, Trump staffer Jason Miller dismissed the investigation as "simply the Democrats' latest attempt to score political points by continuing their witch hunt against President Trump, and everybody sees through it."

What everyone should see through is this feeble talking point.

Rod Blagojevich, former governor of Illinois, gained fame for corruption that exceeded even Illinois standards (his predecessor also wound up in prison). In addition to trying to sell Barack Obama's vacated senate seat, he shook down a children's hospital and threatened the owners of the Chicago Tribune. What was Blagojevich's excuse? He launched a (successful) lobbying campaign for a Trump pardon claiming that his prosecution was "unjust and politically motivated."

Former Brazilian President Luiz Inacio Lula da Silva was convicted of charges of graft and money laundering. His explanation? "There was a pact between the judiciary and the media to remove us from power," Lula told a rally of his supporters in 2018. "They couldn't stand to see the poor rise up."

In 1998, the American first lady claimed that her husband was the victim of a "vast, right-wing conspiracy."

Rep. Duncan Hunter, who was among the very first House members to endorse Trump, pleaded guilty to misuse of campaign funds for a variety of personal expenditures including family vacations. There was tension with Mrs. Hunter when it was revealed that campaign funds were also devoted to romantic weekends in Lake Tahoe with individuals "14, 15, 16, 17, and 18." Hunter described the investigation as a "politically motivated witch hunt." (Trump also pardoned Hunter.)

Rep. Chaka Fattah was sentenced to 10 years in prison for racketeering, bribery and money laundering. He apparently used donor funds to pay down his son's college tuition debt and accepted an $18,000 bribe to help a friend secure an ambassadorial post. What did Fattah say about the investigation? Plenty. It was "unconstitutional" and "unlawful" and, yes, "politically motivated."

Trump is no longer shielded by the Justice Department policy against indicting sitting presidents. He is no longer able to claim separation of powers when Congress asks for documents. He is no longer able to put off the IRS audit.

So, yes, he and his followers will shout "political motivation" and "witch hunt," but it rings tinny now, not just because it's so flagrantly false, but also because it's all they've got.

How Mike Lee Ditched Constitutional Conservatism for Trump

March 5, 2021

I didn't watch much of this year's CPAC. My digestion is sound, but there's no point in taking unnecessary risks. Still, I did note the presence of Sen. Mike Lee, a legislator who styles himself a "constitutional conservative." Lee is the son of a distinguished former solicitor general of the United States, a graduate of Brigham Young University and its law school, and the author of three books on the Founding era: "Our Lost Constitution," "Our Lost Declaration" and "Written Out of History: The Forgotten Founders Who Fought Big Government." That's a lot of losing and forgetting.

But it seems that Lee is the one who has forgotten what the founding was about.

Less than two months have elapsed since Donald Trump committed the most monstrous attack on the constitutional order in 150 years by siccing a violent mob on the Congress as it was attempting to certify the election of the man who defeated him. That came on the heels of attempts to strong-arm the secretary of state of Georgia to "find" enough votes to alter the results, efforts to persuade state legislators to defy the voters and replace their states' electoral college slates in his favor and a protracted effort to discredit the election process itself as fraudulent.

CPAC was the first gathering of Republicans and conservatives since those events. And yet, the "constitutional conservative" Lee did not see fit to mention any of that in his address. He spoke of "leftists who hate the Bill of Rights" and he argued that "faith in government is tyranny." He denounced Democratic governors, who had imposed what he regarded as overly restrictive COVID-19 rules, as tyrants and stressed that "we" (meaning Republicans) "trust the people."

Lee may be sincere in his desire to restore some equilibrium to the separation of powers. He has introduced several bills that would curtail executive authority, and when Trump usurped legislative powers and arguably broke the law by declaring a spurious border emergency, Lee was among a small number of senators who opposed him. But that burst of independence must have exhausted the senator, because at the time of Trump's first impeachment trial, less than a year later, Lee was among Trump's firmest defenders. "What he did was not impeachable," Lee told Politico. "It was not criminal. And I don't think what he did was even wrong."

CPAC was, according to The Bulwark's Tim Miller, a festival of forgetting. If the Capitol insurrection was mentioned at all, it was only to blame it on judges who ruled against Trump's risible lawsuits. Mostly though, the speakers stuck to antifa and imaginary late-night ballot dumps.

If Lee is genuinely concerned about the constitutional order, his highest priority should be the authoritarian turn that the Republican Party has taken under Trump. He might begin with these facts: Nearly two-thirds of the Republican House caucus, along with eight senators, voted not to certify President Joe Biden's election. Seventeen Republican state attorneys general signed onto Texas's preposterous lawsuit challenging the results in Pennsylvania, Michigan, Georgia and Wisconsin. (The Supreme Court tossed it.)

The MAGA crowd stormed the Capitol and erected a gallows, but elected Republicans helped prepare the ground.

Any "constitutional conservative" surveying the wreckage of the post-Trump GOP must be concerned about the state of the people they are so ready to "trust." Can self-government succeed when a plurality of one of the two major political parties no longer even believes in democracy?

A survey of Trump supporters, who number about half the Republican Party, found that not only do they nearly universally believe the fraudulent election lie, but 70% want Trump to serve another term and remain in office—after his second term is complete.

Among Republicans more broadly, 86% opposed conviction and disqualification in the second impeachment trial, and 83% thought the trial itself should never have happened. In other words, not even attempting to subvert the election through improper influence, pressure and, eventually, violence was enough to break their cult-like devotion. Sixty-five percent do not believe Biden was legitimately elected. Nearly 30% of Republicans believe the chief claim of the QAnon conspiracy, that Trump was secretly fighting a cannibal cabal of child-abusing Democrats and Hollywood elites. Half of Republicans aver that antifa, not MAGA supporters, rioted at the Capitol.

Lee waxed indignant about some regulations instituted legally by Democratic governors to deal with a 100-year emergency. Did some go overboard? Maybe. Is that a threat to the Republic? Good God, no.

On the other hand, a significant portion of the electorate is slavishly loyal to a person rather than a party, philosophy or country. A huge number of Americans have had their faith in democracy significantly eroded. A large minority of the population believes pernicious falsehoods and cannot be disabused. And leaders who hold advanced degrees and write books about the founding cannot bring themselves to confront that reality. That seems like a bigger challenge.

J.D. Vance Joins the Jackals

March 19, 2021

The question of what will become of the Republican Party in the post-Trump era seems to be on everyone's lips. A New York Times survey found that Republicans themselves have five distinct views of Donald Trump, including 35% who are either "Never Trump" or "Post Trump." But 65% fall into the "Diehard" camp (27%), the "Trump Booster" faction (28%), or the "InfoWars" segment (10%).

Whatever the future of the Republican Party will be, the shape-shifting J.D. Vance sheds light on the dynamics of how we got here and where the Republican Party is headed. This week, billionaire venture capitalist Peter Thiel announced that he is donating $10 million to a super PAC supporting Vance's potential run for the United States Senate seat from Ohio.

Vance today is a fixture of the Trumpist right, but that isn't the way he debuted. Not at all.

Rarely does a nonfiction book make the kind of splash "Hillbilly Elegy" did in 2016. I was part of the cheering section. Vance emerged as an authentic voice of the working class—a self-styled "hillbilly" no less—to declare that the problems of many working-class people were largely self-inflicted.

Or perhaps a better way to say it is that their problems are a matter of personal choices. Drug abuse, welfare dependency, domestic violence, irresponsible spending and family disintegration were all omnipresent in Vance's family and community. The stories of his upbringing are harrowing. He described his home life as "extraordinarily chaotic." His grandmother once attempted to murder his grandfather by dousing his bed with gasoline and lighting a match (he survived).

In a 2016 interview, Vance told Rod Dreher that his mother probably cycled through 15 husbands/boyfriends during his childhood. Family disintegration was the greatest handicap Vance and others like him were saddled with. "Of all the things that I hated about my childhood," he wrote, "nothing compared to the revolving door of father figures."

His depiction of working-class life wasn't a complete rejection of his origins. He stressed that he loved his family, and that a majority (even if a bare majority) of his community does work hard. For children trapped in dysfunctional homes, one can have nothing but sympathy. And he believed that elites did fail to evince much understanding for people who were struggling. On the other hand, he was keen to counter the pervasive sense of helplessness in the community he was raised in. "There is a lack of agency here—a feeling that you have little control over your life and a willingness to blame everyone but yourself."

In a sense, Vance was the anti-Trump. He was a true son of Appalachia striving to lift his community, in contrast to the faux populist from Manhattan seeking to flatter and exploit them. Vance felt that they needed hope and a generous dose of honesty. Trump offered fantasies and cunningly curated hatred.

During his 2016 book tour, Vance was not shy about his disdain for Trump. When NPR's Terry Gross asked how he planned to vote in November, he said: "I can't stomach Trump. I think that he's noxious and is leading the white working class to a very dark place." And appearing on the podcast I hosted at the time, "Need to Know," Vance recalled texting his editor to say that, "If Trump wins it would be terrible for the country, but good for book sales."

But a funny thing happened after the introduction of J.D. Vance, anti-Trump voice of the working class. He began to drift into the Trump camp. I don't know why or how, but Vance became not a voice for the voiceless but an echo of the loudmouth. Scroll through his Twitter feed and you will find retweets of Tucker Carlson, alarmist alerts about immigration, links to Vance's appearances on the podcasts of Seb Gorka,

Dinesh D'Souza and the like, and even retweets of Mike Cernovich. But the tweet that really made my heart sink was this one from Feb. 12: "Someone should have asked Jeffrey Epstein, John Weaver, or Leon Black about the CRAZY CONSPIRACY that many powerful people were predators targeting children."

By citing the cases of Jeffrey Epstein and John Weaver, one a convicted abuser of underage girls and the other an accused abuser of teenage boys, he is whitewashing the QAnon conspiracy.

Jeffrey Epstein was a despicable creep. John Weaver seems to have done bad things (though he has not been convicted of anything yet). But the QAnon conspiracy teaches that a cabal of leading Democrats and Hollywood celebrities sexually abuses not teenagers but little children, and then eats them. No decent human being should in any way remotely suggest, far less with all caps, that those conspiracies might not be so crazy.

I'm not sure which is worse: that Vance, who just four years ago lamented the rise of conspiracy theories on the right, is now helping to foment one of the worst, or the fact that the Republican base is so warped that ambitious men feel the need to sink into the sewer in search of political success.

Vance's slide from path-breaking writer to Trumpist troll tracks perfectly with the decline of the Republican Party. Peter Thiel clearly believes his new incarnation will win votes. And it may. But to quote Vance back at himself, if he does win, "it will be terrible for the country."

Jonah Goldberg's Narcissism of Small Differences

Oct. 15, 2021

Back in 2016, when formerly distinguished conservatives were suddenly lining up to issue glassy-eyed endorsements of a half-mad reality TV figure, Jonah Goldberg wrote a brilliant column comparing the experience to "Invasion of the Body Snatchers." He captured the sense so many of us had that nearly an entire party and, eventually, nearly an entire intellectual movement had been lobotomized. "People would go to sleep violently opposed to Trump and everything he represented," he recapped for Vanity Fair, "but by morning they'd start telling me how under comrade Trump, we were going to have the greatest harvest we've ever seen." If he does nothing else in his career, I will always cherish him for his indomitability when others, with less to lose, crumpled.

So it's disappointing to see him falling for the narcissism of small differences. As Sigmund Freud wrote, "It is precisely the minor differences in people who are otherwise alike that form the basis of feelings of hostility between them."

Celebrating the two-year anniversary of The Dispatch, Goldberg, apparently feeling the need to do some product differentiation, tossed off a gratuitous swipe at The Bulwark. Both publications are redoubts of Trumpism-defying conservatives and thus, you might think, allies? Compadres? Friends? I was a charter subscriber to The Dispatch.

Regarding The Bulwark, Goldberg said, "If you wake up every morning trying to argue about why Trump is bad and the people who like Trump are evil, you're just as obsessed with him as the people who wake up every morning wanting to prove that Trump is a glorious statesman and everything he does is great." Never Trump and pro-Trump publications, he continued, are "two sides of the same Trump-obsessed coin."

Well. That's awfully close to accusing The Bulwark of Trump Derangement Syndrome—very odd considering that Goldberg has doubtless experienced that aspersion many times himself at the hands of people who regard any criticism of "el jefe" as treason. And completely untrue to boot: The same week Goldberg accused The Bulwark of Trump obsession, the website published pieces about Chris Christie, long-term trends in the American military, Florida Gov. Ron DeSantis, vaccine objectors, California Gov. Gavin Newsom, Russian President Vladimir Putin, Norm MacDonald, the Taliban, President Joe Biden, gender balances in education and election reform, just to offer a small sample.

Recently, responding to a piece by Jonathan Chait, Goldberg again aimed a potshot at The Bulwark, writing:

"Let's say I believe that Trump and his followers, apologists, and enablers are an ongoing threat to democracy. Does that mean I have to support Joe Biden?

"That's the question of the moment for a bunch of people on the left and the right. It seems to be the view of my friend Bill Kristol and many in his circle."

Much depends upon what "support" means. Goldberg implies that Kristol's "circle" (aka The Bulwark) demands uncritical cheerleading for Biden. And Goldberg refuses to compromise his integrity, he says, to get on any partisan's squad. "I want no part of any popular fronts."

Here we have descended several fathoms deep into the narcissism of small differences. It's hard to see what Goldberg is talking about. Throughout the past several months, The Bulwark has published dozens of pieces arguing that Biden should move to the center. Far from a Biden cheering section, The Bulwark has urged that the Democrats thank Sens. Joe Manchin and Kyrsten Sinema for saving them from themselves; that they take the more modest infrastructure bill as a win; and that they make efforts to broaden their appeal to estranged Republicans. Charlie Sykes has pleaded almost daily on "The Bulwark Podcast" for the Democrats to reject the maximalist demands of the progressive wing of the party, comparing it with the Republican Freedom Caucus.

Perhaps it comes down to a matter of emphasis. Kristol has said that in light of the Republican Party's lunatic spiral, he's hoping for Biden's success (while also advising that Biden, you guessed it, tack to the center). I have written that in the Virginia governor's race, I'm voting Democratic because the Republican is signaling his endorsement of the fiction that our elections are not legitimate. Sometimes, you must lean toward one over another, even when it makes you uncomfortable. To attempt to move Democrats toward policies that are centrist and ~~popular~~ and will result in success for the only sane party left at this moment is not to endorse the agenda of Sen. Bernie Sanders. Quite the opposite. And it is not a surrender to partisanship.

Also, it is sometimes the case that when you insist you're not constructively helping one side at the expense of the other, you actually are. As Goldberg himself wrote in 2016: "Politically, anti-anti-Trumpism, as Orwell could have told you, amounts to being objectively pro-Trump, even if it doesn't sound like it."

All of us must grapple with the threat the Republican Party now presents to the country. The Dispatch has insisted passionately that they want to transcend Trump and Trumpism. Don't we all? But even with Trump in gilded exile, the Republican Party continues to spin out of orbit. A glance at the senatorial contest in Ohio is as good a gauge as any that the party is demanding extremism and crack-pottery (neither J.D. Vance nor Josh Mandel is an actual kook; both are simply adapting to suit consumer demand). And there is zero chance that any candidate can withhold the Republican presidential nomination from Trump should he run in 2024, which makes him the de facto leader of the GOP today. So, as Goldberg has himself acknowledged five years ago, it's fantasy to suppose that "the real nuts are the ones who are making a big fuss about how awful he is."

The MAGA Perversion of Patriotism

Dec. 17, 2021

In September, an Arizona student who tested positive for COVID-19 was ordered to quarantine for several days. Seems normal, no? No. The boy's father barged into principal Diane Vargo's office and demanded the kid be allowed back into school immediately. Vargo was alarmed when the intruder told her that others were on their way, warning, "If you keep doing this, we're going to have a big problem." Two other men did arrive, one carrying military-style zip-ties. They told Vargo that they were going to make a "citizen's arrest."

As it happens, the intruders were the ones arrested—by the police.

The same month, in Michigan, a meeting of the Barry-Eaton District Board of Health was disrupted when a man threatened to make a citizen's arrest of a county health official after a school mask mandate was announced. That was mild compared with the death threats Genesee County officials have received over masks. And that, in turn, was less serious than what happened in Kent County, where someone tried to run a health official off the road.

Stories of threats and violence aimed at ordinary Americans who are simply serving on school boards, supervising elections or holding public office are not new. It's a mashup of pandemic-induced mania, social media misinformation, Trump-incited disinhibition and something in the water.

The citizen's arrest has become a theme running through some of the most sinister of the recent plots. It has a long pedigree, originating in English common law. In the U.S., it has been codified in a number of ways by states. But the invocation of the citizen's arrest as an excuse for political violence is new.

Former President Donald Trump set this table with his "lock her up" chants and accusations of treason against anyone who damaged his fragile psyche. His 2019 Twitter tantrum at Rep. Adam Schiff was the gold standard: "I want Schiff questioned at the highest level … Arrest for Treason?"

Back in 2020, when a gang of 14 right-wing nuts plotted to kidnap Michigan Gov. Gretchen Whitmer, they claimed they were effecting a "citizen's arrest." In a normal world, such a claim would be instantly dismissed as risible. But we're not in that world. We're in the world where the sheriff of Barry County, Dar Leaf, seemed to think it had merit. "It's just a charge, and they say a 'plot to kidnap' and you got to remember that," Leaf told a local Fox affiliate. "Are they trying to kidnap? Because a lot of people are angry with the governor, and they want her arrested. So are they trying to arrest or was it a kidnap attempt?"

"A lot of people are angry with the governor," he said. And then, as if the next words flowed logically, he added, "and they want her arrested." Right, because when we dislike the policies of duly elected officials, we arrest them?

The threats are proliferating. The Washington Post reported that lawmakers were subjected to 3,900 threats in 2017. By 2020, that had more than doubled to 8,600, and in 2021, the rate rose even faster. As Tim Alberta noted in his Atlantic profile of Rep. Peter Meijer, the fear factor in Republican politics has changed. Republicans displayed a total lack of political courage in dealing with Trump from 2015 to the present. But because they didn't stand up to him when the consequences would have been merely political, they/we now face a very different climate: fearing for their safety and that of their families. Describing a colleague who said he couldn't vote to certify the 2020 election, Meijer said: "Remember, this wasn't a hypothetical. You were casting that vote after seeing with your own two eyes what some of these people are capable of. If they're willing to come after you inside the U.S. Capitol, what will they do when you're at home with your kids?"

Many members of the Jan. 6 mob didn't conceive of

themselves as coup plotters (in contrast to those in the Oval Office). They thought they were vindicating democracy, not destroying it. As they were storming the Capitol, they were exchanging messages that reflected the treason talk Trump had normalized. "You are executing a citizen's arrest. We have probable cause for acts of treason, election fraud."

There is a substrate of perverted patriotism here. The invocation of the citizen's arrest signifies a wish for legitimacy. They yearn to be responsible citizens, upholding the law and the duties of the individual. They have been corrupted—all the more reason for the rest of Americans to assert their uncorrupted patriotism. They must defend the election workers, health care workers, school board members, journalists, politicians and anyone else who is being abused by the mob. If patriotism animates only the worst among us, we are lost.

Thank God Trump Isn't President Right Now

March 11, 2022

President Joe Biden is not very good at his job, and yet, I thank God every day that Biden is president. In the Ukraine crisis, he has redeemed the hopes of those who voted for competence. The administration's warnings to Moscow were unambiguous without being hysterical. Our revelations of intelligence unmasking Russian disinformation and false flag narratives were on the nose. Biden's coordination with European allies was a skillful presentation of unity (special kudos to Secretary of State Antony Blinken).

There were some missed opportunities. The president should have placed the invasion of Ukraine in a broader historical context and outlined how the struggle between democracy and authoritarianism is the defining issue of our time, whether abroad or at home. And he ought not to suggest or pretend that Americans can be spared any hardship, even higher gas prices, during this fight.

But Biden sees clearly what sort of menace Russian President Vladimir Putin is. Only the most obtuse or twisted soul could fail to see it ... which brings us to the president's predecessor.

A quick refresher on former President Donald Trump's relations with Putin and Ukraine leaves little doubt that far from deterring Putin, he was Putin's most reliable "useful idiot."

Trump wasn't the first president to go soft on Putin, of course. Barack "Tell Vladimir I'll have more flexibility after the election" Obama plowed that ground very well. But at least Obama knew what he was doing. He chose diffidence and called it wisdom. Trump was a dupe and a dope, a walking refutation of the adage "you can't kid a kidder."

At Trump's first meeting with Putin, he accepted the Russian's denials of election interference and announced the creation of "an impenetrable Cyber Security unit so that election hacking, & many other negative things, will be guarded and safe." The plan to let the fox guard the henhouse was dropped after GOP senators exploded.

Trump demanded that the translators take no notes at their meetings, but it is clear from the public record that Trump often repeated Putin's talking points.

At the Helsinki summit, Trump infamously endorsed Putin's version of the election interference story over that of America's own intelligence agencies. Later, speaking to Tucker Carlson, Trump revealed the other ways Putin had been poisoning his mind, planting ideas about NATO countries. "Montenegro is a tiny country with very strong people … They are very strong people. They are very aggressive people, they may get aggressive, and congratulations, you are in World War III." Who believes that Trump had ever heard of Montenegro, far less formed views about their supposed aggressiveness, before that meeting?

Trump got other ideas from his conversations with Putin and dutifully lobbied our major trading partners in the G7 to invite Russia back into the fold. They declined.

In 2019, defending his decision to withdraw troops from Syria and Afghanistan, Trump offered this little potted history about Russia's engagement with that country: "(T)he reason Russia was in Afghanistan was because terrorists were going into Russia. They were right to be there."

As with the other Putin nuggets he regurgitated, Trump said this with perfect ingenuousness.

Throughout his presidency, Trump hinted and blustered about withdrawing from NATO, which would fulfill Putin's dearest wish. When his aides objected that this might be harmful politically, Trump conceded the point, as Carol Leonnig and Phil Rucker report, saying "Yeah, the second term. We'll do it in the second term."

As for Ukraine, Putin gave Trump the idea that it was Ukraine, not Russia, that had interfered in the 2016 election. As New York Magazine reported, "Trump repeatedly told one senior official that the Russian president said Ukraine sought to undermine him." Trump further believed in a mysterious "missing server" that was hidden in Ukraine containing the missing emails. In his infamous 2019 shake-down call with Volodymyr Zelensky, Trump alluded to it: "I would like you to find out what happened with this whole situation with Ukraine, they say CrowdStrike … I guess you have one of your wealthy people … The server, they say Ukraine has it."

In 2016, Trump suggested that Russian ownership of Crimea be recognized and again repeated a factoid that seems likely to have come directly from Putin. "The people of Crimea, from what I've heard, would rather be with Russia than where they were," he told ABC News. The GOP platform was changed to omit endorsing arms for Ukraine.

Trump is a disturbed human being who is constantly revealing his attraction to violence and "strength." Even as Putin was smashing his tanks into Ukraine, Trump fawned over his "genius" and then boasted that "I know him very, very well." He said it was "wonderful." He backtracked after a day or two, but doubtless only after being advised that it was politically unwise.

But if, God forbid, there were ever a second term, political considerations wouldn't be dispositive, and the most sinister and credulous man ever to disgrace the Oval Office would be unconstrained.

Liz Cheney's Star Turn

June 10, 2022

The House Jan. 6 Committee will begin a series of prime-time hearings this week, starting on June 9. For the past 11 months, Rep. Liz Cheney has been the face and the voice of the committee. Like the Greek goddess of retribution, Nemesis, she has brought down her hammer on former President Donald Trump and the Trumpified GOP, delivering blows in the form of truth. As the committee accumulated information, it was she who divulged selected segments to the public. She was the face and voice of accountability.

Last December, Cheney was the one who read out those damning text messages exchanged between Fox News hosts and Trump's chief of staff, Mark Meadows.

She quoted Sean Hannity: "Can he make a statement? ... Ask people to leave the Capitol?" She quoted Brian Kilmeade: "Please get him on tv. Destroying everything you guys have accomplished." She cited texts from Laura Ingraham fretting that Trump was "destroying his legacy." She quoted from Donald Trump Jr., too. Apparently lacking a direct channel to his father, Jr. was furiously texting Meadows, "He's got to condemn this s—. ASAP. The Capitol Police tweet is not enough."

Cheney read these aloud during a committee meeting, and then intoned, "Still, President Trump did not immediately act." There followed more frantic text exchanges with members of Congress afraid for their lives and more urgent pleas from Trump Jr. "It has gone too far and gotten out of hand." Cheney paused again and noted, "But hours passed without the necessary action by the president."

It was Cheney, accompanied only by her father, who showed

up for the House commemoration of the one-year anniversary of Jan. 6. With the exception of the exceptional Cheneys, the entire Republican side of the House was empty on the morning of Jan. 6, 2021. The others were presumably content to pretend that marking the anniversary amounted to using it as "a partisan political weapon," as Kevin McCarthy put it.

It was Cheney who, after the racist atrocity in Buffalo, New York, spoke the truth about the GOP's coddling of the Great Replacement Theory. As recently as 2017, the Great Replacement Theory was the province of neo-Nazis and kooks. When the Charlottesville marchers chanted, "The Jews will not replace us," most people had no idea what they were talking about. By 2022, Tucker Carlson touts the Great Replacement explicitly on his cable show, and Rep. Elise Stefanik, who replaced Cheney as the chair of the House Republican Conference last May, has run Facebook ads incorporating the idea.

Over a reflection of migrants crossing the border in President Joe Biden's sunglasses, one ad reads: "Radical Democrats are planning their most aggressive move yet: a PERMANENT ELECTION INSURRECTION. Their plan to grant amnesty to 11 MILLION illegal immigrants will overthrow our current electorate and create a permanent liberal majority in Washington."

Note the shameless use of the term "insurrection." Always go on offense. Stefanik, like 99% of Republicans, has learned to love aggression, revel in trolling and despise honor.

Cheney responded with unadorned reality: "The House GOP leadership has enabled white nationalism, white supremacy, and anti-semitism. History has taught us that what begins with words ends in far worse."

The Wyoming state GOP chairman, Cheney told Bob Costa, is a member of the Oath Keepers. It's a nightmare from which we never seem to wake. Retiring Rep. Adam Kinzinger, who also agreed to serve on the Jan. 6 Committee over McCarthy's objections, has been similarly honest about the GOP's dalliance with white supremacy and racism.

Kinzinger is not seeking reelection against a Trump-backed challenger, but Cheney is soldiering on. Unseating her is a top Trump priority, and a recent poll found her lagging her challenger by 30 points. Unimaginative people ask, "What's her endgame? She's going to lose, so what was this all about?"

Well, for those who couldn't see it, she has explained what this is about. It's about her love for this "incredible jewel, this incredible blessing of a country." It's about the "danger of this moment." It's about her reverence for the Constitution that several generations of Cheneys have fought to defend. Here is how she explained it in February:

"Republicans used to advocate fidelity to the rule of law and the plain text of the Constitution. In 2020, Mr. Trump convinced many to abandon those principles. ... The Jan. 6 investigation isn't only about the inexcusable violence of that day: It is also about fidelity to the Constitution and the rule of law, and whether elected representatives believe in those things or not."

Those words will ring hollow to the Trumpified GOP who have lost the capacity to love their country more than their party. But for many of us, they rekindle a spark of hope that some leaders will serve as a saving remnant.

Try Trump at the Ballot Box, Not in Court

Aug. 26, 2022

Last week, responding to Damon Linker's persuasive arguments about the dangers of criminally prosecuting former President Donald Trump, I ventured that we might have to sacrifice justice on the altar of prudence. The column provoked a fierce backlash, and while it may seem odd to say this, I'm in sympathy with my critics and offer these reflections in all modesty. I may be wrong. Perhaps the right path is to pursue justice "though the heavens fall." But we cannot pretend that there is no risk to this path. In fact, the stakes could not be higher—the stability of our society—so it's worth considering all of the possible outcomes before barrelling forward.

The prosecute-and-be-damned party believes fervently that any hesitation to hold Trump criminally liable for his crimes amounts to appeasement and cowardly submission to what Michelle Goldberg calls "the insurrectionists' veto."

It's a great point. The very worst part about refraining from prosecuting Trump is that it would seem to be a victory for bullying and intimidation. It is precisely when he acts like a Mafia don or a fascist that the urge to slap him down with every available weapon is strongest.

And yet, that emotional reaction cannot be the whole story. If the point is to vindicate the rule of law, we have to carefully consider what an indictment and trial of Trump would actually look like.

As we've seen in the aftermath of the Mar-a-Lago search, giving Trump a colorable case for "persecution" by the Democrats is a huge gift. There is no point in denying that he has a genius for making himself the center of attention. An indictment and trial would place him back at the center of American life—where he longs to be. His every belch and grunt would be newsworthy, just as it was during his presidential term, and we'd again be trapped in Trump's world.

Confronted with the possibility of a trial on federal charges, Trump would be a Vesuvius of trust-dissolving venom. He would impugn every aspect of the justice system. It will all be "corrupt" and "a disgrace" and "so unfair." The grievance/persecution narrative that he has already germinated would come into full bloom. The country would be transfixed by every piece of evidence, every bit of testimony and every legal argument. No one would speak of anything else. Everyone would choose sides. Those Republicans who might have been inclined to leave Trump behind would be pulled back into his orbit by the centripetal force of the Great Trump Trial.

The right-wing infotainment circuit would transform Trump from a fading former leader into the sacrificial figure who is persecuted for his followers. The Christ imagery favored by his fervent disciples is not subtle. He takes the slings and arrows for conservative, God-fearing, Christian Americans. The search of Trump's home, though thoroughly justified, reignited the fires of Republican fury that had subsided to embers. As recently as early July, half of Republicans were ready to move on from Trump in 2024. But after the raid, the whole party snapped back to cult status, ready to tear down the FBI, the DOJ and more on behalf of their hero/martyr.

Trials are tricky endeavors, and our system (rightly) sets a high bar for conviction. The scope of the offense would of necessity be limited. Lawyers make mistakes, as do judges. And testimony can go awry. Remember the disappointment with Robert Mueller's performance before Congress?

If Trump is to be tried in Florida for mishandling classified documents, can we be confident that a jury of 12 would not include at least one MAGA-adherent? And what if Trump is tried and acquitted? How much stronger will he seem to the base? *Look at everything they threw at me! The Russia hoax. The Mueller investigation. The first impeachment. The second impeachment. And now this communist show trial. And they failed every time!*

The danger of striking at the king and missing is not to be discounted.

If the point is to reify the principle that no one is above the law, consider this: In its current incarnation, the Republican Party is fully capable of nominating someone indicted for a felony. In fact, it seems more likely that Trump would be the 2024 nominee if he *were* facing indictment. As Rep. Liz Cheney remarked, "Large portions of our party, including the leadership of our party" are "very sick." So if a Democratic administration indicts Trump and the Republican Party nominates him anyway, what does that do to respect for the rule of law?

If Trump were to face a criminal trial, all of the anti-Trump energy in the nation would be diverted into rooting for a verdict from 12 Americans—and then hoping that an appeal were unsuccessful, and then that the Supreme Court did the right thing.

Our more urgent task is to make arguments to a larger jury—the American public—that Trump must never be permitted to wield power again.

Chapter Three: Challenging Election Integrity

Thinking Impeachment

Nov. 4, 2016

So I guess the election is not "rigged" after all, eh, Donald Trump? Every possible damaging headline is falling on Hillary Clinton's head as the country staggers toward Nov. 8. So many nets that Clinton appeared to wriggle out of—the alleged influence-peddling while secretary of state, the negligence about classified emails, the dishonesty (including possibly under oath), the kid glove treatment by the FBI—it's all roaring back at the worst possible moment for her.

If she wins (a bigger "if" today than a week ago), it will be due only to the Republican Party's suicidal decision to nominate and support a pathological narcissist/con man—a figure utterly outside the parameters of acceptability for public office. Any public office. So as culpable as Democrats are for nominating a person who ought to have been disqualified, Republicans are even more irresponsible for risking the terrible powers of commander in chief to someone most elementary school kids would regard as emotionally unstable.

Winston Churchill described World War II as the most avoidable war in history. He meant that Hitler's intentions were clear, and that if the allies had summoned the courage to stop him while he was weak, they would have made short work of it. Instead, they dithered and deluded themselves until he was strong, costing the world 50 million lives.

No, I'm not comparing Trump to Hitler, but the parallel is just this: The 2016 election was the most winnable for Republicans since, oh, 1984. The party had gained nearly a thousand federal, state, and local legislative seats since 2008, including control of the House and Senate. Barack Obama's presidency had disappointed even many of his most blinkered admirers. Until 2016 started to make him look good by comparison, Obama's approval rating had been stuck in the 40s (a bad omen for the candidate of his party). Approval of Obamacare, the Democrats' signature initiative, was under water (39.2% approve, versus 48.8% disapprove), and premium hikes were kicking in. The economy has been sluggish, logging one slow quarter after another—permanent second gear.

But, some protest, if it's close and there's a chance to get a (nominal) Republican elected, why not jump on the Trump train? Because there's a second lesson in that Churchill story—namely, that when someone has revealed his character to you, don't delude yourself that he will change.

Trump is the most shameless liar ever to advance this far in American politics. He doesn't lie just about trivial matters like his poll numbers, the size of his crowds or his wealth; he engages in the kind of dishonesty that undermines civic trust. He retweets false statistics about black-on-white crime and about Muslim Americans celebrating on 9/11. He legitimizes crazed conspiracy theories, like that vaccines cause autism; Rafael Cruz was implicated in JFK's assassination; and George W. Bush lied us into war.

Beyond his titanic dishonesty, Trump is appallingly uninformed about foreign and defense policy—the most important (and unconstrained) realm of presidential action. He confused the Kurds with Al-Quds. He thinks NATO is a protection racket and that Japan, South Korea and Saudi Arabia should go ahead and develop nuclear weapons. He plans trade wars. In addition to ignorance, he regularly displays comprehensive antipathy for American values that one would have thought were nearly universal. He threatens war crimes. He applauds the war crimes of others, including those of Saddam Hussein ("He throws a little gas; everyone goes crazy"), and the butchers of Tiananmen Square. He praises Vladimir Putin like a toady.

Trump openly encouraged violence at his rallies and

threatened it at the Cleveland convention when he feared that he would fall short of the required delegates for nomination. That, alone, should have been enough for the party to drop him like radioactive waste. It violated a sacred civic norm that we abide by the democratic process and do not threaten or bully our way to power. His refusal to say that he'll respect the result of the election was part of a well-established pattern.

His defense against the charge of sexual boorishness is ... confirmed boorishness, explaining that the women in question are too unattractive to merit pawing.

Should we elect him and then impeach if necessary? Who, exactly, would we trust to do that—this crowd of Republicans who (with a few laudable exceptions) has fallen into line for him? What would he have to do to merit impeachment if his thousands of offenses did not merit censure, a much lower bar? No, once elected, there will be very few checks on Trump. It's Clinton who should fear impeachment—which might be the best we can hope for at this dismal, dispiriting moment.

The 16 Things You Must Believe if the "Witch Hunt" Accusation Is True

July 14, 2017

One column cannot accommodate the list of things you must believe if you trust that Donald Trump is truly the victim of a baseless witch hunt. Consider this a mere stab.

1) Donald Trump Jr., Paul Manafort and Jared Kushner did nothing wrong by meeting with a Kremlin-connected Russian offering dirt on Hillary Clinton. The emails requesting the meeting specifically mentioned a "Russian government attorney" and added that the requested meeting concerned "very high level and sensitive information" … that "is part of Russia and its government's support for Mr. Trump." That doesn't prove a willingness to collude.

2) Concern about Paul Manafort's extensive links with Vladimir Putin's former puppet in Ukraine, Viktor Yanukovych, including at least $12.7 million in payments, is, to quote Manafort's words, "silly and nonsensical."

3) That Jared Kushner's attempt, during the transition, to secure a back channel with the Russian government using their secure communications equipment in the Russian embassy was not alarming/inexplicable.

4) That Donald Trump's stubborn refusal ever to breathe a critical word about Vladimir Putin, even as he has freely criticized U.S. allies, or acknowledge Russian meddling in our election, is not strange.

5) That Michael Flynn's firing after less than a month on the job was really just because he had misled Mike Pence.

6) That Donald Trump's pressure on James Comey to go soft on Michael Flynn was purely a measure of loyalty and friendship

from a person who has rarely shown those traits before.

7) That Comey's firing, at least according to evolving White House accounts, was due to his mishandling of the Clinton file—no, wait. It was due to poor management of the FBI, which was suffering from low morale—uh, no. It was because of two factual errors Comey made in congressional testimony. Finally, that it was really over the "Russia thing"—but only because Trump was an innocent man frustrated by Comey's unwillingness to clear him publicly.

8) That it was irrelevant that Trump told the Russian ambassador and foreign minister in the Oval Office the day after Comey's sacking that the FBI director was a "nut job" whose removal had relieved "great pressure because of Russia. That's taken off."

9) It's pure coincidence that one of the only foreign policy advisers on the Trump campaign was Carter Page, who was under FBI investigation for Russia ties. In Moscow, he gave a speech denouncing U.S. policy, saying, "Washington and other Western capitals have impeded potential progress through their often hypocritical focus on ideas such as democratization, inequality, corruption and regime change." Anti-anti-corruption isn't disturbing.

10) That White House objections to sanctions against Russia, which passed the Senate 98-2, are purely procedural.

11) That former Manafort partner and Trump surrogate Roger Stone, who boasted about links to WikiLeaks founder and America-hater Julian Assange, and accurately predicted in August 2016 that John Podesta would be next "in the barrel," was just lucky.

12) That statements by Eric Trump and Donald Trump Jr. about Russian financial ties are not revealing. Golf writer James Dodson quoted Eric as explaining in 2014 how the Trump organization was able to get financing for various golf courses even after the Great Recession. "Well, we don't rely on American banks. We have all the funding we need out of Russia. We've got some guys that really, really love golf, and they're really invested

in our programs. We just go there all the time." Donald Trump Jr., who also traveled to Russia frequently, spoke at a 2008 real estate conference and noted that "Russians make up a pretty disproportionate cross-section of a lot of our assets. We see a lot of money pouring in from Russia." When Donald Trump stated, "I have zero investments in Russia," he did not say that Russia had zero investments in him, but we should believe his other claim, "I have nothing to do with Russia."

13) That President Trump's failure to release his tax returns, despite repeated promises to do so, is because he is under audit.

14) That it's unremarkable that presidential spokeswoman Sarah Huckabee Sanders refuses to say whether Russia is an adversary, a friend or a nation about whom we should be wary.

15) That Donald Trump is the first president since 1949 to cast doubt on America's commitment to NATO, but this is overdue and good for the U.S.

16) That Donald Trump's obsessive attacks on "fake news" are not an attempt to inoculate himself against future revelations but just good old-fashioned right-wing hatred of liberals.

Will Conservatives Give Russia a Pass?

April 26, 2019

The conservative media world, along with all but a few Republican members of Congress, are in the process of handing Vladimir Putin his greatest victory yet. They are ignoring the copious evidence in the Mueller report that Russia interfered in our election—and continues to do so. Pace Jared Kushner, it was a whole lot more sinister than a "couple of Facebook ads."

The narrative has now taken hold that the Mueller investigation originated with the Steele dossier. On Fox News, Ed Henry said that the FBI relied on the dossier to "get this whole thing going." Breitbart referred to the debunked "Russia hoax," and a Wall Street Journal editorial demanded to know how "the partisan propaganda known as the Steele dossier become the basis for an unprecedented FBI probe of a presidential campaign …"

As the Mueller report makes clear, and as even the infamous "Nunes memo" of 2018 conceded, the investigation did not begin with the dossier. It began when a foreign government (believed to be Australia) "informed the FBI about its May 2016 interaction with (George) Papadopoulos and his statement that the Russian government could assist the Trump Campaign."

Sixteen members of the Trump campaign had direct ties with Russians or Russian agents, including President Donald Trump. Some of these were benign. Some were not. Paul Manafort was sharing polling information and plans for winning midwestern states with Konstantin Kilimnik, who has ties to Russian intelligence. Is it the received Republican wisdom now that this was not, at the very least, eyebrow raising?

As for Trump's connections to Russia, we now know that

they existed throughout most of the campaign, even as he was issuing tweets like this one on July 26, 2016: "For the record, I had ZERO investments in Russia." And saying that it was crazy to suggest that Russia was "dealing with Trump." In fact, he had been negotiating one of his largest real estate projects ever, for a Trump Tower Moscow, until just the previous month.

But even if the investigation had begun with the Steele dossier, so what? As they say in legal circles: res ipsa loquitur—"the thing speaks for itself." The Mueller report is sober and meticulous. The dossier is hardly mentioned. If Republican partisans skip over the documentation of Russian meddling because they've internalized Trump's sense of grievance, they are disserving the nation.

The Russian interference was and is far more extensive than a few Facebook and Twitter posts, though those were noxious enough. The IRA (Internet Research Agency), an arm of the Russian intelligence services, along with the GRU (Russia's foreign intelligence service), also organized "dozens" of actual rallies, hacked into the computers of the Democratic Party, maliciously spread falsehoods, stoked already existing divisions between Americans of different races and ethnicities and planted malware. More worrying, the report notes that the Russians aimed at actual voting infrastructure:

"Victims included U.S. state and local entities, such as state boards of elections, secretaries of state, and county governments, as well as individuals who worked for those entities. The GRU also targeted private technology firms responsible for manufacturing and administering election-related software and hardware, such as voter registration software and electronic polling stations.

"In August 2016, GRU officers targeted employees of (redacted), a voting technology company that developed software used by numerous U.S. counties to manage voter rolls ..."

The independent counsel did not further investigate these attempts to subvert elections because the "Office understands that the FBI, the U.S. Department of Homeland Security, and the states have separately investigated that activity."

Or perhaps not. According to The New York Times, former Homeland Security Secretary Kirstjen Nielsen wanted to make blocking Russian interference in the 2020 election a top priority. She was warned off by Trump's chief of staff, Mick Mulvaney, who made it clear that the president still regards any mention of Russia as a personal slight.

In a continuation of patterns established under communism, Russia has exerted malign influence on elections in many nations. Throughout the democratic world, they seek to sow the kind of division and distrust they enjoy in mother Russia. Latvia, Lithuania, Estonia, Ukraine, Hungary and other former Soviet captives have been particularly hard hit, but the Russians have also stirred the pot of Catalan succession in Spain, boosted Marine Le Pen in France, and helped Brexit in Great Britain. In 2017, the Netherlands switched to all paper ballots to prevent Russia from hacking its election.

What is the difference between other democracies and the U.S.? Only here does dismissing the threat of Russian interference now equate with loyalty to the president.

Trump Thinks He's Above the Law

Oct. 11, 2019

Donald Trump is testing whether he can claim immunity from the rule of law. That's the plain meaning of the announcement that his administration will not cooperate in any way with the House impeachment inquiry.

The letter released by White House counsel Pat Cipollone brands the impeachment inquiry an effort "to overturn the results of the 2016 election ... President Trump and his Administration cannot participate in your partisan and unconstitutional inquiry under these circumstances." In Trump's words, it's a "kangaroo court."

Nearly everything in that statement is false. Cipollone now joins a long line of sycophants who have offered up their integrity on Trump's altar. "Unconstitutional"? It's hard for something to be unconstitutional when it's explicitly mentioned in the Constitution. Check Article II, Section 4. An effort to undo the 2016 election? Even in the unlikely event that Trump were removed from office, it would be Mike Pence, not Hillary Clinton, who would assume office. Partisan? Half true. Some Republicans have been mouthing Trump talking points, but others have expressed serious concern about Trump's abuse of office. Besides, impeachments have always featured a heavy dose of partisanship. That neither delegitimizes nor explains them. Forty-three out of 45 presidents have managed to avoid impeachment (Nixon resigned) despite ever-present partisanship.

As for the proper body to investigate presidential wrongdoing, as The Washington Post's James Hohmann notes, Trump is arguing that Congress has no authority to investigate him through impeachment and arguing the exact opposite in another case. The

Manhattan district attorney is seeking Trump's tax returns. There, Trump is contending that the court lacks jurisdiction because "the framers" established impeachment as the sole recourse to hold presidents accountable.

Let's consider accountability. We hear constantly that the verdict of the voters should not be lightly overturned. True. But the founders knew power was dangerous, and elections were only one way they devised to prevent its abuse. They divided powers among the branches. They staggered senators' terms to permit some to be more insulated from transitory public passions than others. They devised the Electoral College to prevent the largest states from exercising all the power in choosing presidents and—this is often forgotten—to buffer the judgments of the populace on selecting the chief executive. (The last function of the Electoral College is no longer in use.) And they authorized Congress to impeach presidents and others.

The Constitution refers to "treason, bribery, or other high crimes and misdemeanors," leading many to ask, "Where's the crime?" But there need not be a crime. If the president were to announce tomorrow that he planned to submit all major decisions to Recep Erdogan before acting, it wouldn't be a crime, but few constitutional scholars dispute it would be impeachable.

Declining to abide by lawful subpoenas is a direct challenge to the rule of law. And it is far from the first. Trump has disfigured the pardon power to reward friends. He has twisted trade law into unrecognizable shape, claiming that "national security" required tariffs on Canadian steel. He has declared a state of emergency to fund a notional wall at the southern border—flouting the explicit will of Congress—while acknowledging on the same day that the emergency was bogus. He has expanded the concept of executive privilege to apply to those who've never worked in the White House. He has demanded personal loyalty from career civil servants. He has instructed aides to confiscate Americans' property along the border, promising that if the aides run into legal trouble, he will pardon them later. He told border agents to turn away all asylum-seekers. If an inconvenience, like U.S. law, should arise, they were to say: "Sorry, judge. We don't have the room." He has suggested that guns be taken from people without due process. "Take the guns first," the Red Queen president said. "Go through due process second"—which vitiates the whole concept of due process. And he may even think this is legitimate. Speaking to Turning Point USA in July, Trump said: "Then, I have an Article II, where I have to the right to do whatever I want as president. But I don't even talk about that."

As someone who warned in 2013 about a "dangerous new level of government by decree," I don't need lectures about how it didn't start with Trump. But this level of flagrant norm-shattering and proud lawbreaking demands more than tut-tutting. Along with the shakedown of foreign countries to get dirt on opponents, Trump is demonstrating that he truly believes he is above the law. A nation of laws cannot tolerate that.

There Is No Return to Normalcy

Nov. 12, 2020

The day after the secretary of defense was fired is not a great time for the secretary of state to joke about a transition to a "second Trump administration." If he was, in fact, joking.

I've had conversations in the past few days with people who disliked Trump enough to pull the lever for Biden but still believe that the Republican Party is sound and will snap back to normal now that Trump is defeated.

I'd like to believe that, but the auguries are not good so far. The party's leaders have closed ranks around Trump, repeating the lies and conspiracies he's spinning about a stolen election. They are laying the predicate for the next four years—the stab in the back. Trump didn't lose; he was robbed. Biden is not the president; he's the usurper.

You really couldn't have asked for a more open-handed Democrat than Joe Biden. He has made every effort to soothe the bitterness of our politics and attempted to unify the country. Someone on CNN said he had "slammed" Trump for failing to concede, but that's wrong. He said it was "embarrassing" and wouldn't burnish Trump's legacy—which is about the mildest way to describe what Trump is doing.

But major figures in the Republican Party—from Majority Leader Mitch McConnell to Minority Leader Kevin McCarthy to the head of the Republican National Committee to the attorney general and the aforementioned secretary of state—are playing along with the charade of distinguishing between "legal" and "illegal votes." Republican attorneys general from 10 states have petitioned the Supreme Court to intervene and stop the vote counting in Pennsylvania.

Some Republicans, recognizing that Trump's attempt to discredit the election is his most severe assault on democratic norms yet, are attempting to right the ship, and God bless them. Sen. Mitt Romney was among the first to congratulate President-elect Biden. Sens. Lisa Murkowski, Susan Collins and Ben Sasse have also extended best wishes to the winner. George W. Bush issued a gracious statement, as did a number of governors—Larry Hogan, Phil Scott, Governor-elect Spencer Cox and Charlie Baker.

But McConnell, one of the most influential men in the party, is saying that "President Trump is 100 percent within his rights to look into allegations of irregularities and weigh his legal options" as if this is just a speeding ticket. And McCarthy told Fox News: "President Trump won this election. So everyone who is listening, do not be silent about this. We cannot allow this to happen before our very eyes."

Meanwhile, Rush Limbaugh has laid down the marker for the next four years: "There's simply no way Joe Biden was legitimately elected president." Funny, Rush didn't explain why, if the Democrats were successful in stealing the election from Donald Trump, they didn't also steal it from Sens. Thom Tillis, Joni Ernst, Susan Collins and Lindsey Graham?

The Trump Republicans have gone wading in the fever swamps and invited the creatures to the inner circle. We've always had conspiracy theories, but we've never before elected a conspiracy monger, and we've never before had the minority leader of the House of Representatives as well as a U.S. senator welcoming a fringe conspiracist (Representative-elect Marjorie Taylor Greene).

In recent months, we've learned that 37% of Trump supporters believe that all or parts of the QAnon conspiracy are true, and that 34% of Republicans and Republican learners think the COVID-19 pandemic was intentionally started by powerful people (the figure for Democrats and Democratic leaners was 18%).

Into that warm petri dish for incubating crazy thinking, insert one defeated Trump claiming voter fraud and you get yesterday's new polling showing that 70% of Republicans do not believe the 2020 election was "free and fair."

The difference between 37% and 70% is the difference between a disturbing tendency and a potential crisis of legitimacy.

About 72 million Americans voted for Donald Trump. If the vast majority of them believe—falsely—that the election was stolen from them and that their votes didn't count, what does that do to any opportunity for national healing? How do they respond if the sitting president goes beyond filing frivolous lawsuits and urges state legislatures to submit alternative slates of electors (as Mark Levin has urged)? Or if he asks the military to take to the streets by invoking the Insurrection Act?

Some object that Republicans who are indulging the president's tantrum are merely playing for time and waiting for him to come to terms with reality. That makes no sense. By helping him to stoke the base's paranoia, they are making it less, not more, likely that he climbs down off the crazy tree.

No, the branch of Republicans that brought Trump to power is now attempting to poison the well for sane Republicans in the future. Instead of being able to focus on policy or (gasp) possible cooperation with the Democratic president on urgent matters like the pandemic, the narrative will be set by the grievance machine. The Trump crowds were still chanting, "Lock her up!" in 2020. Is there any doubt that they'll be chanting, "Trump won!" in 2024?

Republicans Must Confess Complicity in the Big Lie

Jan. 19, 2021

If you missed the retraction from the right-wing online magazine The American Thinker, it's one for the ages. Noting that they had received a warning from lawyers for Dominion Voting Systems, the editors admitted that they had published pieces that "relied on discredited sources who have peddled debunked theories ... These statements are completely false and have no basis in fact. ... We apologize to Dominion for all of the harm this caused them and their employees. We also apologize to our readers for abandoning 9 journalistic principles and misrepresenting Dominion's track record and its limited role in tabulating votes for the November 2020 election. We regret this grave error."

Fox News has issued similar retractions. This is the beginning, not the end, of the story. Dominion has sent letters to 20 other entities and individuals, including One American News Network, Newsmax, Lin Wood, White House Counsel Pat Cippolone and Rudy Giuliani. Sidney Powell, the "Kraken" lawyer in Donald Trump's orbit, got more than a warning. She was slapped with a $1.3 billion defamation lawsuit for her outrageous and outlandish claims including that Dominion's voting machines were designed by Hugo Chavez to help him rig elections; that the machines contained secret algorithms to change Donald Trump votes into Joe Biden votes; that Dominion had bribed Georgia officials to obtain its contract with the state; and that she had a video showing the company's founder bragging that his system "could easily change a million votes, no problem."

Powell has yet to grovel as The American Thinker did, but she would be wise to start. Dominion is not backing down. CEO John Poulos told The Washington Post that he would prefer to take these cases to court rather than settle, because "We feel that it's important for the entire electoral process." The company did not rule out suing Trump.

It seems that the only means we still possess as a society for holding people to account for vicious and democracy-endangering lies is the tort law system. The only acknowledgment of wrongdoing in the most destabilizing crisis of the past 160 years was that extracted from an obscure website by a private company whose reputation and income took a severe hit. I wish Dominion every success against the other defendants, but what of the country that has taken a severe hit? Can Dominion also sue Ted Cruz, Josh Hawley, Mark Levin, Rush Limbaugh, Laura Ingraham, The Federalist, the 17 state attorneys general who joined the ludicrous Ken Paxton lawsuit challenging the election results in four states, Kevin McCarthy, the 121 House Republicans and six Senate Republicans who voted to reject the Electoral College ballots of Arizona? Because until we hear confessions and corrections from conservative media, we will continue to inhabit a dark cave as a country.

The 20,000-plus National Guard presence in Washington, D.C., along with smaller forces arrayed in state capitals may, God willing, get us through the inauguration without any further spasms of violence. But unless the propagandists of right-wing media confess and correct the record—unless they forthrightly admit that they spread lies about the election being rigged—the fury they've incited among a huge swath of Americans will continue to endanger the lives of public officials and crack the foundations of this republic.

The lie they propagated is what propelled those deluded people to storm the Capitol. Of course, the perpetrators of the violence are fully responsible for their decisions, and some of them were clearly mentally unbalanced or extremists or criminals of various stripes. But there were also thousands of otherwise normal people who were deceived into believing that their democracy had been fatally compromised, and millions who now harbor doubts about our system's legitimacy. Nearly 75% of Republicans believe that Trump was the legitimate victor of the election. They couldn't have gotten this idea entirely from Facebook posts or YouTube videos (though those platforms bear responsibility, too). No, without the imprimatur of prestige conservative media like Fox and Limbaugh, and the support from official Republican Party organs, and the complicity of actual Republican office holders like Ken Paxton, Kevin McCarthy, Steve Scalise, Josh Hawley and Ted Cruz, it's doubtful that Trump's big lie could have led where it did. The guilt is corporate.

The goons who defiled the Capitol and smashed poles into the heads of police thought what they were doing was righteous. They think of themselves as patriots. The cynical liars like Hawley and Levin and the rest, who took advantage of their ignorance for their own purposes, drape themselves in the flag, too. How dare they? Their little game, which began by indulging the base's attraction to stories like the birther conspiracy, has matured into stoking insurrection. Is there no point at which they question their complicity? Is there no point at which they say to themselves, "For the good of the country, I need to correct this"?

Dominion Voting Systems may get its reputation restored through the courts. The damage to the nation must be repaired by a chastened Republican Party.

Sidney Powell Admits It Was All a Lie

March 25, 2021

The Big Lie is starting to unravel. One of Donald Trump's disinformation stars, Sidney Powell, is backing down. But while we're considering the matter of truth and lies, let's recall when conservatives cared about truth (or seemed to).

In the 1990s, Guatemalan activist Rigoberta Menchu was a phenomenon. Of Mayan descent, she offered harrowing testimony about the conduct of the Guatemalan military during that country's civil war. Her 1983 as-told-to memoir, "I Rigoberta Menchu," was a sensation. In 1992, she was awarded the Nobel Peace Prize.

When it came to light that Menchu had distorted key aspects of her autobiography, right and left responded very differently. David Stoll, an anthropologist, learned through archival research and interviews with more than 120 people that some of her tales were false. A younger brother she said had died of starvation never existed. Another brother, whom she claimed had been tortured to death in front of her parents, died in completely different circumstances. A New York Times investigation confirmed Stoll's findings.

Liberals tended to excuse Menchu, on the grounds that her story revealed a "larger truth." Some argued that while details of her story might not have been strictly true, the overall narrative remained valid because it "raised our collective consciousness" about the Maya people.

Conservatives were appalled that Menchu's Nobel Prize was not rescinded, and galled that some liberals defended Menchu's invocation of "my truth." There was no "my truth" or "your truth" they countered. There was only *the truth*.

The Menchu story comes to mind because this week we've witnessed further evidence of just how corrupted the right has become. The assault on truth is Donald Trump's most damaging legacy.

It's not good for Dominion Voting Systems and Smartmatic that allies of the president grossly defamed them, but it may turn out to be good for the country that they are availing themselves of legal remedies.

Powell, a key propagandist in Trump's big lie about the 2020 election, has issued a response to Dominion Voting Systems defamation lawsuit. Let's review some of the statements Powell made after the election:

Appearing on Newsmax on Nov. 17, Powell said she had a video showing Dominion founder John Poulos bragging, "I can change a million votes, no problem at all." The video did not exist.

At a press conference with Rudy Giuliani and others, Powell said Dominion had been "created in Venezuela by Hugo Chavez to make sure he never lost an election." She said the machines had an algorithm that automatically flipped votes, and that George Soros' "No. 2 person" was "one of the leaders of the Dominion project." Also false.

Her tone has changed.

The reply Powell's lawyers issued to Dominion's complaint is a climb down. After challenging the court's jurisdiction and venue (standard lawyer maneuvers) and adding the claim that her comments were First Amendment-protected political speech, they get to the substance and things get truly mind-bending.

Sure, Powell's reply acknowledges, she made a series of claims about the election being stolen, but because she was clearly speaking in a political context, her comments must be construed as standard political exaggeration.

The election truther's argument, then, is that any factual claim, no matter how false, is insulated from consequences under defamation law if it is connected to politics. This is worse than "my truth." This is the claim that any politically motivated lie is fine.

But Powell takes it to another level. She next argues that the very outlandishness of her false statements is a defense. Sure, her reply acknowledges, Powell had said, "Democrats were attempting to steal the election and had developed a computer system to alter votes electronically." But "no reasonable person would conclude that the statements were truly statements of fact."

So, that's it. The great lie that has poisoned our politics and inspired an attack on the Capitol and bids to become the incubus of future extremism and violence was such absurd bilge that "no reasonable person would believe it."

Of course, millions of Americans did and do believe it. The crazed mob that stormed the Capitol believed every word. Polls have found that between two-thirds and three-quarters of Republicans believe the election was fraudulent.

This is not about Powell or even about Trump anymore. It's about the complete abdication of integrity by leaders on the right—Republican officeholders, conservative opinion leaders, right-wing TV and so forth. At first they countered Trump's lies. Soon after, they began to avoid them. Next, they pretended to find them amusing. Then they shrugged. Finally, they joined. When enough people in authority tell lies, they cripple their audience's capacity for reason. A few meritorious lawsuits cannot repair that.

The Real Steal Is Coming

May 11, 2021

War is peace.
Freedom is slavery.
Ignorance is strength.—George Orwell, "1984"

Welcome to the funhouse world the Republican Party is building. Up is down. Black is white. Lies are truth.

The great cause that Republicans are uniting around is "election integrity." That's rich. The reality is that somebody *did* attempt to steal the 2020 election—Donald Trump. During the days and weeks following his loss, he brayed endlessly that the outcome was fraudulent, laying the groundwork for an attempt to overturn the voters' will.

From the White House, he made multiple calls to local election officials demanding that they find votes for him. He dialed up members of local canvassing boards, encouraging them to decertify results.

At a time when Trump's toadies were calling for legislatures to ignore the popular vote and submit alternate slates of electoral college votes, he engaged in flagrant election interference by inviting seven Michigan state legislators, including the leaders of the house and senate, to the White House on Nov. 20. What did they discuss? You can surmise from their statement issued after the meeting: "We have not yet been made aware of any information that would change the outcome of the election in Michigan and, as legislative leaders, we will follow the law and follow the normal process regarding Michigan's electors ..."

Trump phoned a Georgia elections investigator who was conducting a signature audit in Cobb County and asked her to find the "dishonesty." If she did, he promised, "you'll be praised.

... You have the most important job in the country right now."

The then-president phoned Georgia Secretary of State Brad Raffensperger 18 times. When he finally got through, he wove a tangled theory of voting irregularities that crescendoed to a naked plea to falsify Georgia's vote: "So what are we going to do here, folks? I only need 11,000 votes. Fellas, I need 11,000 votes."

Trump entertained ideas such as declaring martial law, seizing the nation's voting machines and letting the military "rerun" the election. He turned loose his Kraken-conspiracy nuts and his pillow man to spread lies about Dominion Voting Systems, Black-run cities like Philadelphia and Chinese bamboo ballots.

The Trump campaign and its allies filed more than 60 lawsuits challenging election procedures and lost all but one. Pennsylvania was found to have erred in extending the period to fix errors on mail-in ballots. The case was a matter of three days and a small number of votes that would not have changed Pennsylvania's outcome.

And then came the ultimate attack on election integrity—the violent attack on the Capitol and on members of Congress and the vice president as they were fulfilling their constitutional duties.

Leaving no doubt about his intentions for the riot, Trump told a crowd in February that the only thing that prevented the violent mob from successfully hijacking the official tally of the Electoral College votes was the "cowardice" of Mike Pence.

Today, we stand on the precipice of the House Republican conference ratifying this attempt to subvert American democracy. They are poised to punish Liz Cheney for saying this simple truth: "The 2020 presidential election was not stolen. Anyone who claims it was is spreading THE BIG LIE, turning their back on the rule of law, and poisoning our democratic system." In her place, they will elevate Iago in heels, Elise Stefanik, whose claim to leadership consists entirely of her operatic Trump followership.

Let's be clear: The substitution of Stefanik for Cheney is a tocsin, signaling that the Republican Party will no longer be bound by law or custom. In 2020, many Republican officeholders, including the otherwise invertebrate Pence, held the line. They did not submit false slates of electors. They did not decertify votes. They did not "find" phantom fraud. But the party has been schooled since then. It has learned that the base—which is deluded by the likes of Tucker Carlson, Laura Ingraham and Mark Levin—believes the lies and demands that Republicans fight. As my colleague Amanda Carpenter put it, the 2024 mantra is going to be "Steal It Back."

If Cheney must be axed because she will not lie, then what will happen if Republicans take control of Congress in 2022 and are called upon to certify the Electoral College in 2024? How many Raffenspergers will there be? How many will insist, as Pence did, that they must do what the Constitution demands? How many will preserve any semblance of the rule of law and the primacy of truth?

With this sabotage of Cheney, House Republicans are figuratively joining the Jan. 6 mob.

Did the Jan. 6 Coup Fail?

Jan 7, 2022

Jan. 6 should have been the point of no return, the pivot point at which even the most blinkered sugarcoaters of Trumpism recoiled in disgust from what they had wrought.

For everyone who had convinced themselves that, whatever Trump's flaws, the true threat to the American way of life lay on the left and only on the left, Jan. 6 was a blaring klaxon. Yes, he was a buffoon and incompetent and unfamiliar with the levers of power—and yet this clown nearly brought a 244-year-old democracy to its knees.

The most threatening aspect of Jan. 6 was not the ferocious attack on the Capitol but the response of Republican officeholders thereafter. Even after the unleashing of medieval mob violence, 147 Republican members of Congress voted not to certify Joe Biden as the winner of the presidency. The transformation of the GOP from a political party into an authoritarian personality cult became official that day.

In the year since, most Republicans (with some extremely honorable exceptions) have descended further into cultishness. They blocked the creation of an independent Jan. 6 commission, attempted to pack the congressional Jan. 6 committee with Trump Dobermans like Rep. Jim Jordan, and engaged in flagrant gaslighting about the events of that day. Now, with the arrival of the first anniversary of the most shameful day in recent history, Republicans and right-wing opinion leaders have returned to their comfort zone: blame the media.

Former Vice President Mike Pence, who showed uncharacteristic independence that day, has retreated to media bashing. "I know the media wants to distract from the Biden administration's failed agenda by focusing on one day in January," he told Fox News.

Radio host Erick Erickson tweeted that "there is a genuine obsession in the press about it. It was a bad day, but it doesn't outweigh crime, inflation, COVID, school closures, etc. for voters." Erickson was at pains to emphasize that he isn't now minimizing what happened at the Capitol, but merely responding to a "press corps obsessed with it as the worst thing ever."

This is not to say that there's no such thing as press overreaction or hysteria, but the right has been engaging in evasion for years with the "but the media" trope. In the wake of Jan. 6, it looks not just dishonest but absurd. Jan. 6 is not an "issue" like crime or COVID-19 or inflation. It's the heart of our system. Without bipartisan allegiance to the verdict of voters and the willingness to cede power to those you oppose, no other "issues" can ever be addressed.

Encounter Books editor Roger Kimball mocked the gravity of Jan. 6. "Was it an effort to overthrow the government? Hardly." The trouble, of course, is the media: "To listen to the establishment media and our political masters, the January 6 protest was a dire threat to the very fabric of our nation."

In fact, Kimball claims, the media narrative amounts to a "January 6 insurrection hoax" to pair with the "Russia collusion hoax."

Unlike some of those cited above, New York Times columnist Ross Douthat is not an apologist for Trumpism. He doesn't blame the media, but he doubts that Trump has the wherewithal to subvert our system. Yes, Trump did try to steal the election, Douthat writes, but the courts and state legislatures failed to do his bidding.

That's a comforting thought, but it fails to grapple with two things. One is the GOP's systematic purging of officials who did the right thing in the 2020 election. Georgia Secretary of State Brad Raffensperger has been removed from the board overseeing election certification and is being primaried, as is Georgia Gov. Brian Kemp. Across the country, Republican officials who stood in the breach when it counted and did the right thing are being hounded from office. Members who voted to impeach are resigning or close to resigning.

It's true that Trump didn't quite know where the pressure points were last time, but he's learning. He has supported secretary of state candidates who deny the validity of the 2020 result in four swing states. Meanwhile, Republican-controlled legislatures in a number of states have passed laws withdrawing power over election certification from local election administrators and handing it to legislatures.

But the most profound reason to fear a repeat of something like Jan. 6 is that Trump has corrupted the minds of a substantial percentage of Republican party members.

The polls consistently show that about two-thirds of Republicans believe the Big Lie that the election was stolen. Nearly a third believe that "Because things have gotten so far off track, true American patriots may have to resort to violence in order to save our country." Among rank-and-file Republicans, Jan. 6 is not even viewed as regrettable. One poll found that 52% identified those who entered the Capitol as "protecting democracy."

Institutions are not self-sustaining. They are composed of people, and if people have lost faith in them or have given themselves permission to break the rules, they will crumble.

A people deluded and propagandized cannot be trusted to uphold the pillars of the democratic process. Trump failed at his improvised coup, but he succeeded in warping enough of the electorate to make another attempt—and even success—all too possible.

The Trump Coup Is Ongoing

Feb. 4, 2022

Some look back on the events following Donald Trump's 2020 election loss and think we dodged a bullet: *There was a coup attempt, and thankfully it failed.* Others believe that the whole thing has been overblown. Even as evidence piles up that the coup was far more extensive than siccing a mob on the Capitol, those two takes seem unshaken. There is another way to look at it: The coup is ongoing. With every new revelation about how extensive Trump's efforts to overturn the election were—and they are arriving on an almost daily basis—the flaccid response of Republicans makes the next coup that much more thinkable.

Trump, we now know, paged through the federal departments and agencies looking for willing insurrectionists. He explored the possibility of having the Justice Department seize voting machines in swing states (Bill Barr shot down the idea), and then considered installing Jeffrey Clark as attorney general in Barr's place (a threatened mass resignation stayed his hand). He then turned to the military and considered using his emergency powers under the International Emergency Economic Powers Act to permit the Pentagon to seize voting machines and other records. Things had gone as far as the drafting of a presidential "finding" about nonexistent fraud. Trump also tested the waters at the Department of Homeland Security, asking Rudy Giuliani to see whether the (unlawfully appointed) acting deputy secretary, Ken Cuccinelli, would seize the voting machines under that department's auspices. Cuccinelli begged off.

This comes on the heels of revelations about phony slates of electors. Eighty-four Republicans from seven states signed bogus documents claiming that Trump had won their states and sent these fake Electoral College certificates to the National Archives.

Trump was busier attempting to undo the election than he had ever been as president. He summoned the leaders of the Michigan legislature to the White House after the election to convince them to certify that their state, which voted for Biden, had voted for him. He cajoled and threatened Georgia's secretary of state to "find" 11,780 votes. He phoned local election officials to pressure them to say they found fraud, buzzed the Arizona governor repeatedly even up to the minute he was signing his state's certification, and strong-armed the vice president to, in Trump's own words, "overturn the election."

A little-noticed feature of the stories about Trump's thus-far unsuccessful efforts to stage a coup is that even among the MAGA crowd, some things were considered beyond the pale. Barr was willing to swallow a lot, but he couldn't go along with lying about imaginary vote fraud. The high-ranking lawyers at the Justice Department were Trump appointees, but they would resign *en masse* rather than see Clark subvert the department for plainly unlawful ends. Brad Raffensperger voted for Trump but refused to lie for him. Cuccinelli was Trump's loyal immigration hawk, but he couldn't see his way to using his Homeland Security post to confiscate voting machines and commit fraud. And though Mike Pence, pressed hard by Trump for the last full measure of devotion, wavered (he phoned Former Vice President Dan Quayle for advice), in the end, he did what he knew was right.

A healthy body politic, like a healthy physical body, needs antibodies. It needs certain automatic defenses. The actions of those Republicans were the vestigial antibodies of a healthy democracy. The people who made those crucial decisions were acting out of a sense that anything less would be dishonorable and would be perceived as such by the whole society.

But would they make the same decisions today? Every single time a Republican suggests that what Trump did and attempted to do was anything less than a five-alarm fire, they are weakening our immune system.

Sen. Susan Collins was asked whether she could support Trump in 2024. She declined to rule it out.

Just think about what message that sends to the rank and file about what is beyond the pale and what isn't. If Collins might even support Trump, maybe it's not such a big deal.

On the anniversary of Jan. 6, Florida Gov. Ron DeSantis sneered at what he called "nauseating" remembrances, adding that "it's an insult to people when you say it's an insurrection." Another blow to the concept that something truly awful happened that must never be repeated.

Virginia Gov. Glenn Youngkin has not hesitated to appear on the John Fredericks radio show since his inauguration. Fredericks was the host of a rally in October that featured an American flag that had been carried at the "peaceful" Jan. 6 protest. Fredericks also ladles out big helpings of election falsehood to his listeners.

The National Republican Senatorial Committee has announced a new podcast, hosted by Sen. Rick Scott, to help 2022 GOP senate candidates. First scheduled guest: Donald Trump.

It was not just an attempted coup. The steady sapping of republican virtue continues.

Are Democrats Up to Preventing the Next Coup Attempt?

May 20, 2022

In 1980, because I was an idealistic conservative eager to do my bit for democracy, I volunteered for my local Republican Party as a poll watcher. When polls closed, election officials asked us to gather around as they opened the backs of the machines one by one and tallied the votes. We could all see what was happening, and we all gave our assent that the totals were correct.

It was a glimpse into the ordinary yet extraordinary system we've devised over decades and centuries to ensure that elections are performed honestly and securely. Each state has developed its own procedures, but they're all broadly similar. The results of each polling location are delivered to the precinct and then on to the canvassing board. Election administrators are observed by partisans of both parties, and the results are often counted more than once.

Our voting systems in America have not always been perfect—the most glaring flaw being the disenfranchisement of many African Americans until the mid-20th century—but we corrected that, and over time and in most places, we've conducted free and fair elections every two years.

Today, that stability is at risk.

Across the country, candidates who deny the legitimacy of the 2020 election are seeking office in order to prepare the ground for the next election contest. Pardoned Trump ally Steve Bannon is encouraging MAGAites to run for local posts with authority to count votes. Bannon uses his popular podcast to tout "taking over the Republican party through the precinct committee strategy ... It's about winning elections with the right people—

MAGA people. We will have our people in at every level."

At least 23 candidates who deny the outcome of the 2020 election are running for secretary of state in 19 states. Among those are battleground states that Joe Biden won narrowly: Michigan, Nevada, Georgia and Arizona. Trump has endorsed candidates in Georgia, Arizona and Michigan, the only time in history that a former president has bestirred himself over races so far down the ballot. "We're seeing a dangerous trend of election deniers lining up to fill election administration positions across the country," Joanna Lydgate, chief executive of the States United Democracy Center, told The Guardian. States United also tallies 53 election deniers seeking governorships in 25 states, and 13 election deniers running for attorney general in 13 states.

Additionally, death threats and intimidation from MAGA extremists have caused one in five election administrators to say they will leave their posts before 2024. The most common explanation is that too many politicians were attacking "a system that they know is fair and honest" and that the job was too stressful. A February survey of 596 local election officials found that they spanned the political spectrum pretty evenly—26% identified as Democrats, 30% as Republicans and 44% as independents. A majority said they were worried about attempts to interfere with their work in future elections.

While MAGA types are beavering away, attempting to stack election boards and other posts with election-denying zealots, what are other Americans doing? The clock is ticking.

Democrats are likely to have a tough election in November—not that widespread Republican victories will cause election deniers to reconsider their belief that the 2020 race was stolen. But while Democrats are likely to lose seats in the House and Senate, local elections may not be so lopsided, particularly if the craziness of some of these candidates is highlighted. Kristina Karamo, for example, the Trump-endorsed secretary of state candidate in Michigan, claims that she personally witnessed fraudulent vote-counting in 2020, that Trump won her state (Biden won it by 154,000 votes) and that left-wing anarchists attacked the Capitol on Jan. 6.

Some Republicans, it should not be forgotten, continue to uphold the integrity of elections; a handful of honest Republicans saved the country from a potentially disastrous constitutional crisis in 2020.

If past is prologue, Democrats will probably pour money into unwinnable races over the next few months. Remember Amy McGrath? She was supposed to dethrone Mitch McConnell in Kentucky. Democratic donors gave her $88 million. Remember Jaime Harrison? He was going to defeat Lindsey Graham in South Carolina. Donors shoveled $130 million his way. Harrison lost by a 10-point margin. McGrath lost by nearly 20 points. The list goes on. Beto O'Rourke, anyone? (Republicans do this, too. Just look at the money wasted in Alexandria Ocasio-Cortez's district.)

This year, donors are spending millions in an attempt to unseat the execrable Marjorie Taylor Greene. Sigh. Trump won Greene's district with 75% of the vote. This. Won't. Work.

Democrats, independents and sane Republicans should focus instead on the critical local contests that will determine who counts the votes in 2024. Those unsexy races for local positions and administrative posts like secretaries of state could make the difference in 2024 between an election and a coup.

Chapter Four: Getting Cozy With Autocrats

Where Does a Patriot Turn in 2016?

July 29, 2016

Where does a true patriot turn in the 2016 presidential election? The Democratic Party's national convention is attempting to lay claim to the patriot mantle. Yet the party is not quite there. Former Defense Secretary Leon Panetta was heckled with chants of "no more war." The Code Pink wing lost the nomination this year, but it won the platform—and may yet win it all in the next cycle.

President Barack Obama seeded his own speech with patriotic grace notes, and though he recoils from Donald Trump, his horror at Trump's style seemingly blinds him to their similarities. On substance, they are more alike than not. This shouldn't be shocking, considering that Trump has been a Democrat for most of his life. What is stunning is the degree to which so many patriots whose eyes water at the flag and the national anthem imagine that Trump is a patriot in the same mold.

Obama reproached the Republican nominee for wanting to "turn away from the rest of the world." But that's Obama's view, too. He's happier to be a follower than a world leader, never more gratified than when the U.S. is more modest. When asked why he failed to give even rhetorical or moral support to the millions of Iranians in the streets during the abortive Green Movement, his administration explained that the U.S. was tainted by its history and that any expression from us would have backfired.

His refusal to help the suffering people of Syria—failing even to provide a safe haven for refugees, which has had radiating consequences for Europe's stability and security—was grounded in the same perspective, that American power is blundering when it is not downright imperialistic. When he did intervene, as in Afghanistan, it was feckless. In Libya, he played second fiddle to European powers, which seems more morally acceptable to progressives.

Trump thunders that "we don't win anymore" (he's referring to trade, which is completely wrong) and bristled (rightly, in this instance) at the humiliation of our sailors at the hands of the Iranians in January. But like Obama on steroids, he takes a dim view of America's moral standing.

When he was questioned about his warm endorsements of Russian President Vladimir Putin and reminded that Putin has killed quite a few critics, Trump shrugged, "Our country does plenty of killing also." That's an extraordinary calumny, implying not the indisputable fact that we have too many violent deaths in America but that, like Russia, our government engages in targeted assassinations of political opponents. Here Trump leaves Obama behind altogether.

Asked about the attempted coup in Turkey, Trump's tropism toward tyrants was manifest. He praised Turkish President Recep Tayyip Erdogan's success in thwarting the coup, and when asked about Erdogan's crackdown on thousands of journalists, educators, judges, civil servants and others, Trump was unmoved. "I think right now when it comes to civil liberties, our country has a lot of problems," he said. He mentioned Ferguson and Baltimore and police being killed, and he offered this: "When the world looks at how bad the United States is and then we go and talk about civil liberties, I don't think we're a very good messenger."

Trump misses the most crucial fact about Turkey: The thwarted coup may have empowered Erdogan to take one of the world's most advanced countries with a Muslim majority, a NATO ally, down the path of Iran. But also consider his view of America. Is that how a patriot thinks? We lack the moral standing to criticize other nations on human rights?

Trump has infamously praised Saddam Hussein ("He killed terrorists"—no, the opposite), China's communist bosses who mowed down protesters in Tiananmen Square ("They put it down with strength") and even Kim Jong Un, about whom he said: "You got to give him credit. ... He wiped out the uncle. He wiped out this one, that one. I mean, this guy doesn't play games."

But Trump has reserved his greatest affection for Putin. Yes, George W. Bush praised Putin (once), but he wised up. Yes, Obama attempted to "reset" relations (less explicable), but he was forced to backtrack when Putin snatched Crimea, reintroduced Russia's military directly into Syria and made proxy war on Ukraine.

Trump is on notice about all of that and much more. It is common knowledge (which is not to say Trump knows it) that Putin's opponents tend to die by poison and other methods beloved by the KGB; that state-controlled Russian media ceaselessly incite America hatred; that Russian internet trolls seek to destabilize democratic governments in Europe and quite likely here; that Putin sides with Iran, Bashar Assad (Syria's genocidal dictator) and Hezbollah; and that Putin, having strangled civil society and freedom in Russia, seeks to recapture the lost glory of the Soviet empire. Yet Trump bats his eyes at Putin like a schoolgirl with a crush.

Part of Trump's appeal is chauvinism—a strutting sort of nationalist appeal (unsupported by anything approaching policy ideas). It's more than odd, then, that his followers are unshaken by his willingness to be Putin's poodle.

Why Would You Want Putin as a Friend?

July 21, 2017

Leaving aside the question as to whether there was actual collusion between the Trump campaign and the Russian government during the 2016 election, it is undisputed that candidate Donald Trump was eager for a friendship between our two nations. The most recent accounts of the president seeking out more one-on-one time with Putin at the G-20 dinner—using only a Russian translator—is the latest evidence that this enthusiasm is undiminished.

President Trump has offered scores of comments about Vladimir Putin over the past four years, many times leaning over backward to doubt whether Putin was really guilty of assassinating reporters and opposition figures. Had Putin "been found guilty," Trump demanded. On many occasions, Trump gushed that Putin was "very nice" to him, and praised the dictator's "strength." On May 5, 2016, he told Fox News' Bret Baier, "I know Russia well. I had a major event in Russia two or three years ago—Miss Universe contest—which is a big, incredible event, and incredible success ... And you know what? They want to be friendly with the United States. Wouldn't it be nice if we actually got (along) with somebody?"

Perhaps this is a generalized wish for international peace. But if so, why didn't Trump show similar benevolence toward China? Instead, throughout the 2016 cycle, he repeatedly promised to label China a currency manipulator and threatened to impose high tariffs on Chinese imports.

You have to overlook a lot to imagine that Russia's intentions toward the United States and the West are benign.

Consider that Russia has blocked eight United Nations

resolutions condemning Syria's use of chemical weapons. Russia was tasked, in an agreement the Obama administration blundered into, with overseeing the destruction of Syria's chemical weapons stockpile. As recently as April 2017, Bashar Assad gassed civilians with Russian connivance. In 2016, Gen. Phil Breedlove, supreme NATO allied commander for Europe, testified before Congress that not only was Russia not targeting ISIS (a favorite fantasy of Putin fans in the U.S.) but it was also intentionally bombing hospitals and other civilian targets in Syria to frighten more refugees into fleeing the country and swamping Europe. Thus has Russia "weaponized" the creation of refugees to destabilize Europe.

Anything that undermines the legitimacy of free and democratic nations in the West is guaranteed to get Russian support. Putin sows distrust and chaos, and he has shown himself willing to use "disinformation"—an old Soviet technique—as well as financial support for extremists of both left and right. Russia supports rightists, such as the Jobbik party in Hungary and the National Front in France, as well as left-wing parties, such as Podemos in Spain and Syriza in Greece.

The Russians have stood solidly behind their ally Iran, even selling the Islamic Republic sophisticated S-300 surface-to-air missiles in 2016, which would make any attack on Iran's nuclear facilities by Israel or the U.S. much more militarily risky.

On state-run media in Russia, the West, and particularly the United States, is portrayed as corrupt, hostile to Russia, expansionist and treacherous. The Russian television channel RT, which used to be called Russia Today but elected to drop the truth in advertising, traffics in conspiracy theories. The 9/11 attacks, it implies, were actually the work of the U.S. government. The Malaysian civilian aircraft shot down over Ukraine (which a Dutch-led investigation found was downed by Russians) was actually targeted by another mysterious plane. The United States, according to RT, is losing its democracy as a corporate elite takes over the country. The CIA is responsible for undermining Ukraine, and so forth. The ceaseless propaganda is having an effect. The percentage of Russians who have a "bad" or "very bad" opinion of the United States has risen from 34% in 2012 to 60% today.

The West's intelligence services are also favorite bugbears of Russian media. As Paul Gregory recounts, "Virtually every truckers' strike, miners' protest or critical Facebook posting is a CIA, U.S. State Department or Germany BND operation" according to Putin.

Above all, Putin's aim is to undermine our trust in one another and in the possibility of knowing the truth. As he told RT journalists in 2015, the Kremlin's goal is to break what he calls the "Anglo-Saxon monopoly on global information streams." He pollutes Western traditional media with lies and laces social media with suspicion and hatred.

It makes you wonder: Why would we want good relations with such a figure?

Historic Snooker

June 15, 2018

The headline writers adore the word "historic." It was ubiquitous in reporting on the April meeting between Kim Jong Un and Moon Jae-in. Kim shook Moon's hand and then guided him over the military demarcation line to step onto North Korean territory. This prompted swoons. What rot. If that was a bona fide gesture of peaceful intent, time will tell. In the meantime, let's assume it was a stunt.

So, too, with the summit between Kim Jong Un and Donald Trump, though in this case the media hype couldn't compete with Trump's own. He has basked in talk of a Nobel Peace Prize and predicted that he and the butcher of Pyongyang were "going to have a great discussion and a terrific relationship." Obviously panting for a meeting, Trump was reportedly livid with national security adviser John Bolton, whose May comments about a "Libya solution" to the nuclear weapons problem apparently spooked Kim into withdrawing from the summit. Trump insisted that it was he who cancelled, just as he did with the Philadelphia Eagles' White House visit.

But he showed quite a lot of ankle in his note. "I felt a wonderful dialogue was building up between you and me," he cooed, closing with words conceding that it was Kim, not Trump, who had actually cancelled. "If you change your mind having to do with this most important summit, please do not hesitate to call me or write." Kim reeled in his catch. He sent an oversized letter Trump could pose with, grinning like a winner of the Publishers Clearing House sweepstakes.

Why is our president smiling? You can always argue that democratic leaders must treat with dictators and even villains of various stripes for the sake of winning a war or securing the peace. You can even argue that sometimes presidents flatter unsavory leaders to build trust and ease tensions. But no historical comparisons can illuminate Trump's ricochets between hysterical threats ("fire and fury") and pusillanimous praise ("very talented") without any substantive change on the part of the dictator. What has changed since the State of the Union address in which Trump honored the memory of Otto Warmbier and detailed the atrocities of the North Korean regime? In gratitude for the exchange of pleasantries, the release of a few hostages and vague offers of "denuclearization," Trump has made himself Kim's doormat.

As a matter of substance, the Singapore summit achieved less than nothing. It was a profound defeat for U.S. world influence and for democratic decency, arguably the worst summit outcome since Yalta. Kim promised to consider "denuclearization," exactly as his father and grandfather had done repeatedly over the past several decades—breaking their promises each and every time. For this puff of cotton candy, Trump agreed to halt "U.S. war games" (using the North Korean term for joint military exercises with South Korea), which Trump himself called provocative! He invited Kim to the White House. He also issued the risible tweet announcing, ahem, peace in our time: "There is no longer a nuclear threat from North Korea."

It's difficult to determine just how stupid Trump thinks the American people are. But there is no question that Trump's affection for strongmen and thugs, evident before in his praise of the Chinese murderers of Tiananmen and his warm words for Vladimir Putin, Rodrigo Duterte and Xi Jinping, has now extended to the worst tyrant/killer on the planet. Trump did far more than overlook Kim's atrocious human rights abuses; he became Kim's PR man: "He's a very talented man, and I also learned he loves his country very much." He has a "great personality" and is "very smart."

Trump granted Kim's legitimacy: "His country does love him. His people, you see the fervor. They have a great fervor."

In 2014, a United Nations report concluded that North Korea's crimes against humanity "entail extermination, murder, enslavement, torture, imprisonment, rape, forced abortions and other sexual violence, persecution on political, religious, racial and gender grounds, the forcible transfer of populations, the enforced disappearance of persons and the inhumane act of knowingly causing prolonged starvation."

What of all that? Trump is understanding, even impressed. "Hey, he's a tough guy. When you take over a country—a tough country, tough people—and you take it over from your father, I don't care who you are, what you are, how much of an advantage you have. If you can do that at 27 years old, I mean, that's one in 10,000 that could do that. So he's a very smart guy. He's a great negotiator."

What was Trump's chief argument in 2016? The U.S. had been the victim of "bad deals" with other countries and he was the great deal-maker. He fingered the Iran deal as the worst deal in history. His defenders will excuse the truckling to Kim as a clever gambit to extract concessions. But Kim has offered absolutely nothing. All of the concessions have come from the United States, including the most crucial one: We've put ourselves on the same moral plane as North Korea. That's what Make America Great Again has achieved.

Trump's Fatal Attraction

March 1, 2019

The good news is that the Trump-Kim summit in Hanoi, Vietnam, did not result in a deal—because any deal would have been nothing but a scam perpetrated by Kim Jung Un. Selling this same rug repeatedly is a North Korean specialty. The Kim dynasty inked agreements to denuclearize in 1985, 1992, 1994, 2005, 2007 and 2012. You've seen the results. Pyongyang violated every one and marched inexorably toward nuclear weapons and ballistic missile technology. It's bad enough to confront the prospect of a nuclear-armed North Korea. It would be worse to, in effect, subsidize it, which is all that was on offer.

Why would Kim give up his nukes? To get American aid to improve his economy? Fantasy. He runs a prison state that actually exports slaves to countries such as China, Kuwait and Qatar. His goal is not to develop the economy but to remain firmly in power and conquer South Korea. He saw what happened to Muammar Gaddafi when he gave up his nuclear program and to Saddam Hussein, who only pretended to be working on one.

That much must be obvious to Donald Trump's advisers, if not to Trump himself, who seemed so eager for a deal that he announced before the Hanoi summit that the U.S. was dropping the demand for a full accounting of North Korea's nuclear weapons and ballistic missile programs. If that sounds precisely like what President Barack Obama did vis-a-vis Iran, it should.

For now, Trump has sidestepped the trap Kim prepared. While he may have avoided one bad outcome, his behavior was so bizarre and sycophantic toward Kim personally that he still departs Hanoi trailing a stench of shame.

There is just no mistaking it: Our president gets excited in the presence of dictators. Appearing with Kim at a press conference, the president warned reporters, as he never has regarding the leaders of democracies, to show respect to Kim: "Don't raise your voice, please. This isn't like dealing with Trump." Trump himself went way beyond diplomatic niceties, favorably contrasting Kim with other "rich kids" who didn't turn out so well.

Even if Trump could overlook the millions who have been persecuted (it's a crime to visit a South Korean website), starved, tortured and worked to death in the "hermit kingdom," it's beyond appalling that he would offer a pass on the torture and murder of a young American, Otto Warmbier. Recall that in 2017, Trump had said, "Otto's fate deepens my administration's determination to prevent such tragedies from befalling innocent people at the hands of regimes that do not respect the rule of law or basic human decency." But off-teleprompter, Trump demonstrated his characteristic sympathy for dictators caught behaving badly. "He (Kim) tells me that he didn't know about it, and I will take him at his word. … I don't believe he knew about it."

Nor did he believe Mohammed bin Salman knew about Jamal Khashoggi's murder. And he took Vladimir Putin's word over the judgment of U.S. intelligence agencies about alleged Russian interference in the 2016 election.

Philippine President Rodrigo Duterte has launched a vicious program of state-sanctioned murders of suspected drug addicts and dealers. According to the Philippine National Police, the state has killed more than 5,000 people since Duterte's election in 2016. Others estimate that the true number is closer to 20,000. Amazingly, Duterte does not dispute this. "What is my fault? Did I steal even one peso? … My only sin is the extrajudicial killings." On another occasion, he said: "Hitler killed 3 million Jews. Now there are 3 million drug addicts. I'd be happy to slaughter them all."

The world is full of misery, and American leaders sometimes

have to deal with unsavory characters. But nothing required President Trump to pick up the phone in 2017 and say to Duterte: "You are a good man. ... I am hearing of the unbelievable job on the drug problem. Many countries have the problem, we have the problem, but what a great job you are doing and I just wanted to call and tell you that."

Explaining the need for a wall on the southern border, Trump offered this odd report from a conversation with China's Xi Jinping, who apparently told the president that China has no drug problem because they employ the death penalty. He found this exhilarating. "If we want to get smart, we can get smart," Trump said. "You can end the drug problem, can end it a lot faster than you think."

It would be less disturbing if Trump's chief weakness were for porn stars and money. Alas, his attraction to thugs seems even stronger.

What's Missing from Trump's China Policy

May 24, 2019

The Dow plunged 450 points on the opening bell May 6 in response to this presidential tweet: "The Trade Deal with China continues, but too slowly, as they attempt to renegotiate. No! The 10% will go up to 25% on Friday." Economists eye this brinkmanship fearfully. Bank of America/Merrill Lynch's global research team, among many others, has warned that a trade war could cause a global recession. Desmond Lachman of AEI notes that there are splash back effects of imposing harsh tariffs. They may succeed in weakening China, but any "marked slowing in the Chinese economy is bound to have spillover effects on those economies with strong trade links to that country."

Among those countries with "strong trade links" to China would be ours. Lachman is warning that Trump's policies may be undermining the strong economy, and that this should worry him looking at 2020. But before we get there, spare a moment to savor the irony of what Trump's policies have so far achieved on one of his favorite 2016 hobbyhorses—the trade deficit. In 2016, the goods and services trade deficit with China stood at $309 billion (which Trump frequently exaggerated to $500 billion). As of March 2019, the trade deficit with China was $379 billion—a 23% percent increase.

As nearly every economist will attest, trade deficits are not important. Between 1980 and 2009, U.S. employment rose when the trade deficit went up and fell when the trade deficit came down. Hmm. Same thing seems to have happened in the first two years of the Trump administration. Employment and trade deficits are both up. Someone should tap Trump on the shoulder and mention this. Actually, don't bother. Gary Cohn talked himself blue in the face on the subject to no avail. Trump is frequently the embodiment of the joke: "Don't confuse me with the facts. My mind is made up."

This is not to say that China should be free to cheat with impunity. But Trump doesn't seem to be focused on the most serious threats from China. He seems fixated on the great crime China commits by selling us products, rather than on the threat to privacy and civil liberties China's authoritarian government represents to its own citizens and to the world.

China's communist government has permitted free enterprise (to a point) and we all know what a massive difference that has made for the average Chinese person. More than 800 million people lifted themselves out of poverty once the state stopped forbidding it.

But in other respects, China has remained as ruthless a Big Brother as Orwell imagined. The internet is successfully smothered by what techies call "The Great Firewall of China." The press is controlled. In Xinjiang province, up to 3 million ethnic Uighurs and other Muslims have been shipped off to concentration camps. Transgressions that can result in deportation include observing Ramadan, growing a beard or phoning relatives abroad. While in camp, they are "reeducated." In March, after U.S. citizen Ferkat Jawdat met with Secretary of State Pompeo, his mother, aunt and uncle were moved to a camp and then sentenced to eight years in prison as retaliation for Jawdat's meeting.

But even for those not physically imprisoned, China is erecting a virtual cage for everyone, with cameras equipped with facial recognition software now ubiquitous, "free" health checks that permit the government to collect fingerprints and DNA, mass surveillance by police and neighborhood snitches, and a system that would make Winston Smith cringe: the "social credit system." This permits Big Beijing to keep tabs on every phone call, text message, jaywalking ticket and night out with too much drinking. If you transgress, you get demerits, and these can be used to deny plane tickets, jobs or apartments. Sometimes the state requires that a special ringtone be added to the miscreant's phone so that he/she will be embarrassed every time the phone rings in public.

That's only a sampling. Equally worrying is China's success in exporting this sinister system as part of its "Belt and Road Initiative."

The Trump administration has very recently begun to impose limits on technology transfers to Chinese tech firms. But the effort has been slapdash. (In 2018, the Commerce Department imposed sanctions on Chinese telecom company ZTE only to see Trump reverse the decision).

Trump is focused on the non-threat of Chinese exports while ignoring the true threat of China's totalitarian system reaching abroad. A few weeks ago, CBS censored a comedy that mocked China's censorship. That ought to worry us more than imported washing machines.

US Blocks Examination of Crimes Against Humanity

Dec. 13, 2019

It's easy to treat Kim Jong Un as a figure of ridicule. I've done it myself. His foreign ministry issues statements like this: "If any language and expressions stoking the atmosphere of confrontation are used once again on purpose at a crucial moment as now, that must really be diagnosed as the relapse of the dotage of a dotard."

His youth, his odd haircut, and his rotund physique don't signal menace so much as clownishness. But that's a mistake. He is, in fact, guilty of crimes against humanity on a massive scale, and the United States government has just chosen to block a United Nations Security Council session that would take up those atrocities.

Remember the North Korean army defector who dashed to freedom across the DMZ in 2017? He was shot several times in the shoulder and back. The regime takes it very personally when people attempt to flee the "socialist utopia." Officer Oh Chong-Song survived. When South Korean doctors operated on him, they found parasites—some 10 inches long—swarming his intestines. This is common among North Korean defectors. Oh said later, "Most of the North Korean soldiers are hungry all the time." Though they are entitled to 750 grams of rice daily, the allotment is often less, because higher-ranking military officers steal and sell it.

Chronic hunger is mild compared with what prisoners and other enemies of the state endure. Human Rights Watch, the United Nations Human Rights Commission and the U.S. Department of State, among many others, have documented the reign of terror presided over by Kim, his father and his grandfather. It would be instructive for President Donald Trump to page through those accounts. Here are some highlights of the 2016 report commissioned by the International Bar Association:

—A prisoner's newborn baby was fed to dogs before her eyes.

—A prisoner's pregnancy was aborted by three guards standing on a plank on her stomach.

—Prisoners caught digging for edible roots were shot.

—Prisoners were tortured and killed for professing religion. Guards were told to "wipe out the seed of Christianity."

—Thousands of prisoners, including children, have been intentionally worked and starved to death.

At the start of his administration, Trump issued wild threats to destroy North Korea utterly; to rain down "fire and fury like the world has never seen," which sounded eerily like the threats Kim himself issues. Trump may have frightened the dictator—he certainly alarmed many Americans—but the next act was even more bizarre, a fawning courtship. "At least," said the eternally hopeful, "they're talking!"

Trump believes that bromide more than anyone, repeatedly boasting of his great relationships with foreign leaders (usually autocrats). He speaks of "falling in love" with Kim Jong Un. He appears to believe that his personal relationship with Kim can overcome the fundamental facts about the regime—that it rules by terror at home and maneuvers by terror abroad. Trump's minions mouthed terms like "denuclearization," as if Kim and kin had not agreed to and broken countless previous pledges. The U.S. canceled military exercises with South Korea, repealed some sanctions previously ordered and showered the dictator with encomia. Trump blandly waved away Pyongyang's missile tests, explaining: "These missiles tests are not a violation of our signed Singapore agreement, nor was there discussion of short range missiles when we shook hands. There may be a United Nations violation, but … Chairman Kim has a great and beautiful vision for his country, and only the United States, with me as President, can make that vision come true. He will do the right thing because he is far too smart not to, and he does not want to disappoint his friend, President Trump!"

A "great and beautiful vision for his country."

Two full-dress summits and one kiss-and-drive at the DMZ, and where are we? North Korea continues to test missiles, manufacture nuclear fuel, threaten its neighbors and abuse its suffering population. In the last few days, it has also reprised threats to the U.S., warning that if progress is not made by Dec. 31, Kim will resume testing long-range ballistic missiles and might have an unpleasant "Christmas gift" in mind for America.

Demonstrating his enduring affection for strongmen, Trump's response has been feeble. By blocking the U.N. from shining a light on North Korea's crimes, Trump conveys his desperation for something he can tout as a breakthrough—and squanders America's moral authority.

Trump Always Had a Whiff of Fascism

Jan. 15, 2021

Throngs of self-styled conservatives and Republicans have now reached the thunderous realization that Donald Trump is not just a harmless clown. Former White House Chief of Staff Mick Mulvaney acknowledged to Chuck Todd that Trump's rhetoric was incendiary, but insisted that this kind of incitement was par for the course in politics, and he was shocked that people took Trump literally.

It seems we have an entire party stocked with Captain Renaults.

While it's good to see some lines being drawn at long last, it may be too late. As with the response to the coronavirus, timing is everything. Republicans had many, many chances to curtail the spread and isolate the superspreader, but they kept saying there was nothing to Trumpism, or it would simply go away, or it was all a hoax perpetrated by the left to install socialism.

I like a conversion as much as the next person, but sorry, there was always a whiff of fascism about Trump. Don't tell us you're just discovering it now. His fascination with strength instead of values, his promises to commit war crimes, his twisted admiration of strong men, his avalanche of lies, his ignorance of and contempt for law, his targeting of minority groups, his stoking of grievance and victimhood. It was all there. Yes, it was interspersed with humor and entertainment. Think that means it can't be dangerous? Have you ever seen a Hugo Chavez or Rodrigo Duterte speech?

Didn't Republicans see him encouraging violence among his followers at rallies in 2016? Don't they remember the thuggish threats his people issued during the 2016 campaign?

In April 2016, Trump and Ted Cruz were still battling for delegates. Trump's recently pardoned consigliere, Roger Stone, alleged (falsely) at the time that he had proof Cruz's victories were all based on "massive voter fraud." Threatening "days of rage" in Cleveland, Stone continued: "We're going to have protests, demonstrations. We will disclose the hotels and the room numbers of those delegates who are directly involved in the steal."

Stone didn't even bother to clothe his threats of physical violence in humor.

Trump was always clear about his attraction to political violence. Speaking of Clinton, he warned that if elected, she could curtail gun rights. "If she gets to pick her judges, nothing you can do, folks." The crowd booed. He then added: "Although the Second Amendment people—maybe there is, I don't know."

That became a tick. He would invoke the Second Amendment as a code for encouraging his supporters to resort to violence. "LIBERATE VIRGINIA," he tweeted in 2020, "and save your great 2nd amendment. It's under siege." "LIBERATE MICHIGAN!" Trump screamed from his keyboard. Heavily armed protesters showed up at the Michigan Statehouse.

Even after some members of that mob were arrested for plotting to kidnap and possibly assassinate the governor and blow up the capital, Trump continued his incitement against Gov. Gretchen Whitmer. Appearing at a rally in Michigan, he joked about the attempt on her life.

Let that sink in. The FBI had arrested a group of domestic terrorists who were planning an attack on a sitting governor, and the president of the United States made light of it: "I'm the one, it was our people that helped her out with her problem. I mean, we'll have to see if it's a problem. Right? People are entitled to say maybe it was a problem, maybe it wasn't."

Did Mick Mulvaney & Co. miss that? Did they not notice when Trump loyalists cheered on vigilantism? When rioting broke out after the George Floyd killing, Trump lapdog Rep. Matt Gaetz tweeted, "Now that we clearly see Antifa as terrorists, can we hunt them down like we do those in the Middle East?"

Perhaps today's "aware" Republicans were otherwise engaged when Trump and his gang made Kyle Rittenhouse a hero, and offered a Republican Convention speaking slot to the gun-brandishing lawyers from St. Louis? What did they make of Trump's tweet, "When the looting starts, the shooting starts"?

Even his famous boast about the loyalty of his followers was revealing. He said he could "shoot someone on Fifth Avenue and not lose any followers." As we now see, he might gain some.

Since Republicans said hardly a word, one must conclude that they were not alarmed when Trump phoned the Georgia secretary of state and instructed him to "find" 11,780 votes—in other words to steal the election he was accusing his opponents of stealing. As historian Timothy Snyder put it, "Post truth is pre-fascist."

Republicans who are drawing a line now and saying that they never imagined Trump's personal militias would smash cops' heads with fire extinguishers and defecate in the halls of the Capitol must also answer this question: What else do you expect when you falsely allege a stolen election? Faith in elections is the sine qua non of a functioning democracy. If elections are not free and fair, what alternative is there to violence?

Now Mulvaney and Nikki Haley and Lindsey Graham and Mitch McConnell and many others are finding a line they think is too far. Inciting a mob to invade the Capitol in order to stop the certification of the election is the one thing, the only thing, that got their attention. Good for them. But while they and nearly the entire Republican Party and its opinion-shaping satellites were averting their eyes, cooperating and enabling, the Trump virus spread. It's now an epidemic, and there is no vaccine on the horizon.

Communist China's Family Values

June 4, 2021

The Chinese communist government is going to permit three children per family. How nice. Here's how The New York Times put it: "The announcement by the ruling Communist Party represents an acknowledgment that its limits on reproduction, the world's toughest, have jeopardized the country's future."

To describe China's "one child policy" as "limits on reproduction" is like calling Jim Crow laws "limits on political participation." The Times account, which at least used the word "brutal" after the jump, also featured a sidebar timeline of China's population policies that was even more anodyne. In 1978, it informs readers, the central government "approves a proposal in which family planning offices encourage couples to have one child, or at most two."

"Encourages"? Not quite. The one child policy deserves to be chronicled among the vicious human rights outrages of our time. Millions of women were strapped to hospital gurneys and had their unborn children torn from their wombs against their will. Millions more were forcibly sterilized. Were they encouraged? Sure. People got stars on little plaques showing how well they'd abided by family planning policies. They also lost their jobs, were denied education and had their houses demolished and their property confiscated if they gave birth to a non-state-authorized baby.

Forcibly aborting eight- and nine-month fetuses was common, as was infanticide. In her unblinking documentary "One Child Nation," Chinese American filmmaker Nanfu Wang interviewed party officials, relatives and midwives who testified to their own acts. One midwife, now 85, said she exclusively helps infertile couples now to "atone" for all the babies she killed in her career. "The policy was from the state," she said. "But I was the executioner. My hands trembled as I did it."

Another family planning official who also participated in countless forced sterilizations, abortions and infanticides recalled that as their babies were taken from them, the women would "scream, cry, go crazy. Sometimes they'd run away and we'd have to chase them down."

Discarded female newborns were left in markets —"their bodies covered in maggots"—on hillsides and in trash heaps under bridges. Delivery men, bus drivers and others who were on the move would regularly find babies in bags by the roadside. Because of the Chinese preference for male offspring (when women marry they are considered members of their husband's family), millions upon millions of couples killed their female babies in hopes of trying again for a son. Even Nanfu Wang's mother tells her that when she went into labor with Nanfu's younger brother, they had a basket waiting if it turned out to be another girl. The abundance of abandoned infants gave rise to a vast human smuggling operation, in which babies were passed to brokers who sold them to orphanages for international adoptions. Eighty percent were female.

Family planning authorities used Cuban-style neighborhood watch committees to spy on couples who were suspected of hiding pregnancies. Workplaces required women to record their menstrual cycles. If couples did flout the laws and raise their unauthorized children, they were forced to keep the existence of these children a secret. Children born outside of the quotas have no legal status, no identity papers, no access to schools or clinics.

The poor suffered the most from the one child policy because the rich could afford to pay fines for unauthorized babies or bribe local officials into looking the other way. The bribes became so lucrative for family planning bureaucrats that they strenuously resisted the central committee's 2016 policy change to permit two children.

The Communist Party, which thinks of Chinese people as

pieces to be moved around a chessboard, not as rights-bearing individuals, is concerned about the future workforce, and the aging population, and so has increased the child quota to three. Each of those millions of only children has two parents and four grandparents to care for—they call it the 4-2-1 problem—and while the official propaganda promised that the state would take care of the elderly, pensions are inadequate.

The Communist Party's social engineering has created a society poor in siblings, cousins, or aunts and uncles. The imbalance between men and women consigns millions of men to permanent bachelorhood. Human Rights Watch has documented "bride stealing" from Myanmar to China.

Many on the American left initially applauded China's one child policy. In 2008, Thomas Friedman said the policy "probably saved China from a population calamity." Others acknowledged that China went too far, but believed that population control was a fundamentally beneficial development. That was a grave error.

While the right was once the province of China skepticism, it has lately taken a turn toward stupidity and xenophobia. Republicans boast of hawkishness toward China, which consists of third-grade taunts like "China virus" and "Kung flu," along with tariffs paid by Americans. But the Trump years featured hardly a whisper about China's gross violations of human decency, and in fact, Donald Trump praised the Uighur concentration camps.

This week's announcement regarding family policy reminds us that China's worst crimes have always been committed against its own people.

What Orban's Apologists Reveal About Themselves

Aug. 13, 2021

As someone who was weaned on stories of leftist intellectuals and journalists traipsing off to communist countries to pay obeisance, I can only shake my head as a parade of right-wingers are making their way to Hungary to sing the praises of authoritarian Viktor Orban. Tucker Carlson of Fox News is the highest-profile rightist to make the trek, but the path was already well-trod.

Former National Review editor and Margaret Thatcher speechwriter John O'Sullivan has moved to Budapest to head the Danube Institute, a think tank funded by Orban's government. He likes his nationalism straight up.

A few years ago, at the National Conservatism conference in Washington, D.C., Orban was an honored guest, which was a bit head-snapping for those inattentive to the drift toward authoritarianism on the right. Speakers at the conference (and a follow-up one held in Rome) have featured mainstream figures such as John Bolton, Chris DeMuth, Peter Thiel, Oren Cass and Rich Lowry. In addition to Orban, other questionable invitees included Marion Marechal (she has dropped Le Pen from her surname) and Steve Bannon pal Matteo Salvini.

I'd wager that all of these conservative opinion leaders, along with more recent pilgrims traveling to Budapest (Dennis Prager, Rod Dreher and Patrick Deneen) are deeply versed in the sad and reprehensible pattern of Western intellectuals becoming seduced by leftist authoritarian regimes. From Lincoln "I have seen the future, and it works" Steffens to George Bernard Shaw to Noam Chomsky to Norman Mailer to William Sloane Coffin, intellectuals have fallen into this trap repeatedly since the 1930s. Paul Hollander's 1981 book "Political Pilgrims" was updated numerous times because intellectuals never tired of finding new autocrats to worship. When the Soviet Union was no longer viable as a model (purges, show trials, the Hitler/Stalin pact and all that), the eager acolytes switched to Mao Zedong and then to Fidel Castro and then to Daniel Ortega (Sen. Bernie Sanders, we're looking at you). Los Angeles Times columnist Robert Scheer even wrote glowing praise of North Korea's Kim Il Sung.

As any number of conservative critics observed, you can tell a lot about people's hierarchy of values by the regimes they admire. Leftists were so focused on equality of condition that they were willing to overlook or whitewash the brutal repression of individual rights. Basics of liberal democracy like free and fair elections, freedom for workers to organize, free speech, free association, religious liberty, property rights and more were virtually nonexistent in those nations. Yet that didn't dim the enthusiasm of the Susan Sontags and Ramsey Clarks.

The ironic plot twist was that the communists never delivered the equality and widespread prosperity they claimed. They didn't even do as well for workers as the "running dog capitalists." And at their worst, the communists starved and shot scores of millions of people. As George Orwell put it, the communist world was "a boot stamping on a human face—forever." It was revealing that so many leftists were willing to sacrifice the precious rights we enjoy—a free press and trial by jury, for example—on the altar of equality.

The American Orbanistas are likewise revealing themselves. Though they are familiar with the folly of political tourism, they are lining up now to laud a leader who no longer even pretends to be democratic. The new state Hungary is building, Orban said, "is an illiberal state, a non-liberal state." Freedom House agrees. It no longer lists Hungary among the world's democracies.

Fidesz has used its control of the judiciary to hound competing political parties with fines and investigations. Orban has also taken control of 80% of Hungary's news media, and these crony-controlled outlets now constitute an enormous propaganda machine. Voting, which never had a long history in Hungary, was hamstrung by gerrymandering to give Fidesz a huge advantage. As The Economist noted, "In the general election last year, Fidesz won 67% of the parliamentary seats—maintaining its supermajority—while taking just less than half of the popular vote." At the start of the COVID-19 pandemic, Orban was granted sweeping powers to rule by decree. The newly empowered state immediately made spreading "misinformation" a crime.

Orban's nationalism is appealing to American conservatives. You can sense their excitement when he says things like: "We do not want to be diverse. We do not want our own color, traditions and national culture to be mixed with those of others." The trouble for the American Orbanistas is that Hungary, a central European nation of 10 million, is not diverse. The United States is and—this cannot be stressed too often—always has been. The "conservatives" who thrill to talk of a monoculture are not preserving an American tradition; they are seeking to import something else.

The leftist intellectuals who lent their prestige to vicious regimes discredited themselves in the eyes of conservatives. We said they were apologists for anti-democratic ideas and justifiers of repression. We said their infatuation with unchecked power was a worrying sign. Every word of that is true today of the conservative pilgrims, who, one would have thought, had more attachment to the American experiment in ordered liberty than to the lure of blood and tribe.

Putin Apologists Disgrace a Fine Heritage

Sept. 16, 2022

At the moment when freedom-loving people around the world are elated (if on tenterhooks) at the progress of Ukrainian forces in pushing back the Russian invaders, Heritage Action, the political arm of the conservative Heritage Foundation, has joined with other self-styled conservative groups to oppose helping Ukraine fight for its life. I know, I know, the Trumpification of the GOP has been a fact for six years, and yet this heel turn is remarkable. It's as if People for the Ethical Treatment of Animals announced that they support puppy mills for medical research.

The pro-Putin, pro-authoritarian voices in the GOP are not yet a majority—about a quarter of House Republicans and 11 of 50 Senators voted against the $40 billion aid package for Ukraine in May—but they're not a small minority either, and the wind is at their backs. CPAC has all but canonized Hungary's strongman Viktor Orban, and in the first hours after Putin rolled into Ukraine, Trump reveled in the murderer's "savvy" and "genius." The 2022 election could bring more authoritarian-friendly Republicans to Congress, and meanwhile, hatcheries of conservative orthodoxy like Fox News and The Federalist are doing the spade work of persuading the base that Kremlin propaganda is more trustworthy—pravda, if you will—than The New York Times.

Just two weeks ago, Tucker Carlson, Putin's favorite American broadcaster (clips from his show are routinely featured on Russian state TV), told viewers that Biden's steadfast support of Ukraine was absurd: "Biden is calling for an unconditional surrender from Vladimir Putin. Here's the weird thing: By any actual reality-based measure, Vladimir Putin is not losing the war in Ukraine."

Poor timing. But that's the least of it. It was bad enough to excuse Putin before February 24 on the risible grounds that he represented some sort of Christian champion and scourge of wokeness. But after? That a spokesman for a so-called conservative TV network can cheer the rape of a free country (Carlson has said he "roots" for Russia to win) is not just morally depraved, it violates the basic tenets of what used to be conservatism. American conservatives once believed that freedom was our most precious inheritance. We were friends to all freedom-loving people and foes of all tyrants. Speaking on the 40th anniversary of D-Day, Ronald Reagan said this to the aging soldiers who had scaled the cliffs of Pointe du Hoc:

"You were here to liberate, not to conquer, and so you and those others did not doubt your cause. And you were right not to doubt. You all knew that some things are worth dying for. One's country is worth dying for, and democracy is worth dying for, because it's the most deeply honorable form of government ever devised by man."

Now it's goodbye to all that apparently. J.D. Vance, Trump's hand-picked candidate for an Ohio Senate seat has said he doesn't care one way or the other what happens to Ukraine. The Federalist denounces Mitch McConnell (who traveled to Ukraine to show support) and other "swamp creatures" for putting Ukraine's security needs ahead of America's. The vapidity of this new "conservatism" is bottomless. They haven't bothered to consider that brutal aggression by a larger against a smaller state invites a Hobbesian international disorder in which no one is safe.

A number of Republicans have seized on the talking point that Biden is more concerned with Ukraine's border than with our southern border. Blake Masters, the Peter Thiel-conjured Republican nominee for senate in Arizona, sneered that America's leaders are "buffoons who hate you so ... they'll keep defending Ukraine's borders while turning their backs on ours." Rep. Mary Miller and her ilk found this irresistibly witty and repeated it.

As if thousands of would-be immigrants attempting to cross the Rio Grande for work represent a comparable threat to tanks and missiles destroying cities, murdering men, women and children, creating millions of refugees, and cutting off food and electricity. This talk of "invasion" of our southern border was always hyperbolic, but to cling to it at a time when our screens are full of images of a true invasion becomes vile.

These supposed conservatives are strangers to the most important themes of traditional conservatism. They dishonor the name. Conservatism was a worldview intimately bound up with opposition to tyranny. Of course we fell short of our aspirations from time to time, but love of freedom was in our DNA—or so it seemed. Our hearts were with oppressed peoples from Lithuania to Tibet to Tehran. We cheered the fall of the Berlin Wall because the USSR was a comprehensive, seven-decade assault on human dignity. We hated it for its repression of speech, thought, religion, movement and enterprise. We hated it for its torrent of lies.

Putin's Russia differs from the USSR in ideology, but in repression and rapacity, it is comparable. And it's scarcely believable that the "useful idiots" who make excuses for it today—who actually root for its success—are "conservatives."

China's Torment Is a Reminder of What We Have

Dec. 2, 2022

In 2022, the United States conducted its 117th consecutive peaceful election (though the aftermath of the 1860 election was not). The 2022 elections were blissfully uneventful, with losers conceding gracefully.

To call that a relief is a tremendous understatement, but this is no time to drop our guard. Trust in democracy remains weaker than it has traditionally been. A World Values survey, for example, found that fewer than 30% of millennials rate living in a democracy as "essential," compared with 70% of their grandparents.

Prominent conservatives like Tucker Carlson openly lionize Hungary's Viktor Orban, and hardcore rightists admire Vladimir Putin. Even mainstream publications can seem to lose sight of what authoritarian rule really means. The New York Times, for example, published a comparison of economic opportunity in China versus the United States under the headline "The American Dream is Alive. In China."

People in democratic countries often fantasize about "being China for a day" in order to achieve their policy goals. So, at this moment, when thousands of Chinese are protesting throughout the nation, we need to remind ourselves of just how terrible unfreedom is. Did we make mistakes in the way we handled a once-in-a-century pandemic? Of course. But we have a free press and disbursed, decentralized power through our federal system and independent courts. Accountability, while imperfect, is built into the system.

In China, by contrast, the ukase is issued by the ruler. We

have mechanisms for self-correction. The Chinese system does not. One party. One ruler.

The overflow of frustration and rage we are seeing today throughout China regarding Xi Jinping's "zero COVID" policy started with an apartment fire in the city of Urumqi. Ten people died and others were injured. Fires happen everywhere of course, but in this building, the fire escapes were locked.

People in Europe and North America protested when their local governments closed schools and businesses for a time, but China's COVID lockdowns are different in kind, not in degree. Videos from the spring and summer showed people screaming from their apartments in Shanghai. In other cities, people imprisoned in their apartments have posted heartbreaking videos. A distraught father said his children had not eaten in three days. In Xi'an, a heavily pregnant woman was denied entry to a hospital because she hadn't been tested recently enough. She went into labor on the street. Her 8-month-old fetus was stillborn. Children, including babies, who test positive can be removed from their parents' care and confined to quarantine centers. In China, if you are even in the same apartment complex as someone who tests positive, you can be forcibly quarantined.

Don't complain. It's unpatriotic to question the wisdom of the party. Nor is the regime embarrassed by its repression. Drones patrol the skies broadcasting this message: "Please comply with COVID restrictions. Control your soul's desire for freedom. Do not open the window or sing." You will learn to love Big Brother.

In the first year, it seemed that China's harsh lockdowns along with testing and tracing kept the total number of COVID deaths down. But China went all in on "zero COVID." While most nations vaccinated as rapidly as they could manage, China declined to purchase the U.S./German mRNA shots. They insisted on using a domestically produced Sinovac vaccine, which is significantly less effective. Large numbers of China's elderly population (numbers are hard to come by) are unvaccinated, which leaves them vulnerable as new, more contagious variants of

COVID are spreading.

Whereas most of the world is emerging from the COVID pandemic, China's bad decisions have left it still in the throes. Infection rates are climbing, the economy is slowing, and after three years of cruel measures, the people are fed up.

Xi is in a bind now. If he relaxes the harsh lockdown measures, many Chinese, lacking either natural immunity or vaccination, will die. If he relents in the face of widespread protests, he will empower the protesters. If he doesn't bend, the frustration and anger will only grow.

The protests have become about more than COVID restrictions. People are chanting, "We want freedom!" in cities throughout the country. They hold aloft white sheets of paper to symbolize the regime's scrubbing of truth. They chant, "Step down, Xi Jinping. Step down, Communist Party." At universities, students speak hopefully of "freedom of expression, democracy and the rule of law." They even echo a declaration from America's revolution: "Give me liberty, or give me death."

The future is veiled in shadow. We remember the glorious demonstrations of 1989, the similar slogans and the inspiring hope for democratic reform. And we remember well the vicious massacre that followed. We can't know how this latest eruption of protest will end. But we can remind ourselves that China, and authoritarianism more broadly, is not the answer to anything.

Chapter Five: Embracing the Extreme

Ross Perot's Lessons for Today

Sept. 2, 2016

In "Fiddler on the Roof," the milkman Tevye imagines what life could be like in "If I Were a Rich Man." Among the shrewder lyrics is the insight that "the most important men in town will come to fawn on me" and pose questions that would "cross a rabbi's eyes." Why? Because "when you're rich, they think you really know."

One cannot guess how much credibility Donald Trump gains through his reputation for business acumen, but it's safe to say, quite a lot. He trades, both in entertainment and in politics (if there's still a distinction), on his reputation as a tycoon, which may be one reason for his refusal (despite pledges) to release his tax returns. Trump's "brand" is everything. When Tim O'Brien authored a book questioning Trump's net worth, Trump sued him and, after lengthy litigation, lost.

Americans have always revered successful businessmen, but you might suppose that after the Ross Perot experience, they'd have acquired a bit of skepticism about the sort of wealthy men who elect to parachute into presidential races.

On paper, Perot was far more suited to the Oval Office than the reality TV star who currently bestrides the Republican Party. Perot was raised in modest circumstances, served honorably in the U.S. Navy, married his college sweetheart, started his own business (Electronic Data Services), received a medal for Distinguished Public Service for his efforts to secure the release of U.S. prisoners of war in Vietnam, and personally organized and sponsored the rescue of two EDS employees who were held hostage in Iran. He sold his business to GM for $2.5 billion, so he was a bona fide billionaire.

He had a straight-talking style. Neither Democrat nor Republican, he disparaged the intelligence of all elites and leaders. His favorite putdown, delivered with a West Texas drawl, was: "Not too smart." He would get "under the hood" and fix the country, he vowed. The wag who quipped "He's a self-made man who worships his creator" could have had Perot in mind.

That's not to say that Perot lacked public spirit. He was concerned about illegal immigration. He worried about our national debt and deficits. The nation probably owes some of the seriousness about budget balancing that characterized the 1990s to him. He favored easels and white boards for making his points—assuming that the public was interested in the details of policy.

But there was another side to Perot which came into focus as his campaign unfolded. He was no economic genius. People presumed that because he was rich, he "really knew." But his chief bugaboo, after deficits, was NAFTA. He famously predicted that if the free trade deal were signed, there would be a "giant sucking sound" of jobs leaving the U.S. for Mexico. It was signed, and in the years following its enactment the U.S. enjoyed an economic boom, creating roughly 2 million jobs a year for six years starting in 1994. (Some jobs were lost, but on net the economy thrived.) Canada and Mexico benefitted as well, with Mexico's economy expanding enough to diminish the tide of illegal migrants seeking to cross the U.S. border. Mexico now purchases more U.S. goods than Brazil, Russia, India and China combined.

It's odd that people who've done well in business should imagine that commerce is unhealthy. This paranoia—a pull-up-the-drawbridge approach to the world—is the red thread that links the Perot and Trump worldviews and campaigns.

Perot's populist appeals were eventually upstaged by his erratic behavior (he dropped out of the race and then jumped back in) and peculiar obsessions. Like Trump, Perot was a devotee of conspiracy theories. He believed that the U.S. Defense Department was running a vast guns and drug smuggling enterprise throughout Latin America and Southeast Asia. He was sure that Vietnam had sent a gang of Black Panthers to kill him and his family, and that Texas drug smugglers had targeted him as well. He attributed his abrupt withdrawal from the presidential race to a plot by President George H.W. Bush to disrupt his daughter's wedding.

Belief in conspiracies conveys at best poor understanding and at worst mental instability. Trump has displayed the same weakness, endorsing the "vaccines cause autism" myth, the "Obama born in Kenya" canard, the "Clintons killed Vince Foster" rumor, the "Rafael Cruz involved in the JFK assassination" nonsense and many more crackpot theories. Worst and most pernicious are the conspiracies he conjures himself—that the "system is rigged," that thousands of American Muslims celebrated 9/11 but the footage has been suppressed, and that if he loses it can only be due to fraud.

Republicans were relieved in 1992 to see Perot unmasked as unstable. Perhaps, after 2016, they will fall out of love with addled businessmen forever.

Is the Party of Lincoln Now the Party of Lee?

Aug. 18, 2017

This year will mark my 30th anniversary as a syndicated columnist. During these years, I have written more words than I would have preferred about race. But race is America's great moral stain and unending challenge. I've tackled school choice, affirmative action, transracial adoption, crime, police conduct, family structure, poverty, free-enterprise zones and more.

Some of those columns took the left to task for maliciously accusing Republicans of racism. A missive on "JournoList," an online forum of left-leaning journalists started in 2007, plotted strategy for how to defend Barack Obama from the taint of Rev. Jeremiah Wright. Spencer Ackerman advised, "If the right forces us to either defend Wright or tear him down ... we lose the game they've put upon us. Instead, take one of them—Fred Barnes, Karl Rove, who cares—and call them racists."

A chapter in my book "Do-Gooders" detailed the shameless calumnies deployed against, among others, George W. Bush. Bush was tarred as sympathetic to the Klan because a vicious lynching happened while he was governor of Texas—though he signed the death warrant for one of the killers and demonstrated great sensitivity on racial issues throughout his career. Examples of such cynical and libelous tactics are unfortunately abundant.

That said, in the era of Donald Trump, I stand slack-jawed as some on the right live down to the worst calumnies conjured from the left's febrile imagination. That the entire Republican Party has not risen up, en masse, to renounce Donald Trump's comments about Charlottesville is a disgrace. Nancy Pelosi's response to the attack on Steve Scalise showed far more decency than did Trump's to Charlottesville. She denounced the would-be assassin and proclaimed that Republicans and Democrats were members of one American family.

Contra Donald Trump, the Hitler Youth wannabes who paraded through Charlottesville last Friday night are not sincere Republicans falsely accused of being Nazis. *They are the real thing.* It should have been the most basic act of American civic hygiene to condemn and anathematize them. (Some Republicans did.) But since it seems we must state the obvious: The "Unite the Right" organizers, including alt-right leaders Richard Spencer and Jason Kessler, advertised their demonstration with Nazi-style imagery, carried torches reminiscent of Nuremberg and Klan rallies, and chanted "Blood and soil" and "The Jews will not replace us." The next day, they clashed with counter-protesters and one of them committed a savage act of ISIS-style terrorism, crashing his car into a crowd. He murdered one person and wounded 19 others, five critically.

Yet Trump's Monday condemnation, if you can call it that, was tardy, stilted and almost immediately withdrawn by his fiery Tuesday press conference. True to his pattern of peddling "alternative facts," Trump insisted that "not all of those people were supremacists by any stretch … you take a look … the night before, they were there to protest the taking down of the statue of Robert E. Lee." I've taken a look. How does "the Jews will not replace us" convey benevolence? Sorry, but people of goodwill who oppose removing the statue of Lee were not in attendance last weekend. Any honorable opponent of iconoclasm would have been repelled by the fascist flags, the slogans, the military gear and the murderous violence.

I am unsentimental about statues of Robert E. Lee myself. He made war on this country to preserve one of the worst forms of abuse known to man. During the Civil War, when he captured black Union soldiers, he re-enslaved them. When it came time for prisoner exchanges, Lee refused to exchange African American Union soldiers for Confederate prisoners. Gen. Ulysses Grant responded that in that case, there would be no further prisoner exchanges.

President Trump's lawyer has circulated an apologia for the Confederate general, arguing that there was no difference between Lee and George Washington. "Both saved America," he wrote. Here's what Grant concluded about Lee 130 years ago: "He fought long and valiantly and had suffered so much for a cause, though that cause was, I believe, one of the worst for which a people have ever fought, and for which there was the least excuse." Those who oppose toppling statues should at least bear the burden of suggesting alternatives—such as erecting monuments to Frederick Douglass ("who's done an amazing job and is getting recognized more and more").

The Republican Party under Donald Trump has regressed from the party of Lincoln to the party of Lee (who, as a historical matter, is actually a skeleton in the Democrats' closet). Hanging racism around Republican necks is the fulfillment of the dearest wish of the left, and unless powerfully rebutted by however many decent Republicans still exist, will discredit the party for years to come.

It Wasn't All Steve Bannon

Dec. 13, 2017

Republican politics was starting to feel like a version of Mel Brooks' "The Producers." In the play, two scammers devise a tax write-off scheme in which they will make a killing by losing money on a Broadway show. They reach for the most grotesque, tasteless musical the human mind can conceive—"Springtime for Hitler"—and are undone when it's a surprise hit.

Roy Moore could have sprung from the imaginations of Democratic operatives hoping to find the embodiment of every stereotype that liberals cherish about conservatives. Ignorance? In a July radio interview, the anti-immigration hardliner couldn't say who the Dreamers are or what DACA refers to. He did not know that the U.S. Constitution, which he purports to revere, forbids religious tests for public office. In the Republic of Moore, Muslims would be barred from serving their country.

Conspiracy monger? He trafficked in the birtherism about Barack Obama and suggested that parts of the Midwest are ruled by Sharia law.

Anti-gay? Moore is not just a traditionalist who opposes same-sex marriage; he wants to put homosexuals in prison, and claims that the U.S. is the focus of evil in the modern world for permitting gays to marry.

Irresponsible? Moore was twice removed from office for failing to obey the law.

Anti-Semitic? When your wife defends against the charge by saying, "One of our attorneys is a Jew," it's not a good sign.

Racist? Anti-woman? Here's where the Moore show veered into wild satire territory, or would have if we hadn't actually seen it unfold. Moore said he agreed with Trump about making

America great again. When, exactly, a voter asked, was America at its greatest? "I think it was great at a time when families were united, even though we had slavery, they cared for one another," said the dolt Steve Bannon chose as the kind of Republican who would stick it to Mitch McConnell and the establishment. Remember how we all spat out our coffee when Joe Biden accused Republicans of wanting to put black folks "back in chains"?

As for women, Moore was the Democrats' jackpot—a supposedly religious conservative flamboyantly fulminating against immorality who was himself a child molester. You could not write this as fiction, because it's too incredible.

In the aftermath of Doug Jones' victory, many Republicans are saying they "dodged a bullet" because if Moore had been elected to the Senate, Democrats would have used him to discredit the entire Republican Party.

Their relief is understandable but premature. Though the morning-after commentary has tended to focus on Steve Bannon's noxious role, the Moore candidacy was not his responsibility alone. A number of key Republicans—Richard Shelby, Mitch McConnell, Mitt Romney, Mike Lee, Cory Gardner and others—treated Moore as radioactive, but an amazing percentage were willing to say that a sleazy bigot was fine as long as he would vote for the president's agenda. Prominent "family values" conservatives such as James Dobson, Tim Wildmon and the infinitely flexible Jerry Falwell Jr. stood by their endorsements of Moore. Sean Hannity issued what seemed to be an ultimatum to Moore to give an account of himself regarding the teens he dated/molested, but then, Obamalike, backed away from his own red line. He said the people of Alabama would judge (as they certainly did, but not in the way Hannity was presumably hoping). Other Fox News hosts returned to the Clinton well again and again, implying that if Bill Clinton hadn't been held responsible for Juanita Broaddrick, well then …

And of course, Moore's most crucial booster was Donald Trump, someone with more than a passing interest in the "he denies it all" defense. The Republican Party has not dodged him, and cannot. You can scan the exit polls of the post-2016 elections so far and draw a scary 2018 picture for Republicans. African Americans, who weren't motivated to turn out in off-year elections even when President Barack Obama implored them to, showed up in force in Alabama. Suburban educated voters—the key to Republican general election victories—have turned against the party in formerly swing state Virginia, and even in reddest Alabama.

The Republican Party has voluntarily donned a fright mask that the hapless Democrats and the evil mainstream media could never have pinned on them. It is probably too late to avert the reckoning that is coming, but even if only as a gesture of civic hygiene, individual Republicans might wish to make clear that the Molotov cocktail politics that Trump brought to the Oval Office is not what they represent.

The Conspiracy Mindset

Jan. 26, 2018

I am old enough to remember when conspiracy theories were primarily the province of the left.

In the 1990s, the San Jose Mercury News ran a series asserting that the crack epidemic in African American neighborhoods was a plot orchestrated by the CIA. The tale was satisfying to many who were predisposed to see the CIA as a villain and who were sympathetic to explanations of addiction that excluded human weakness. The Nation of Islam expressed outrage. Sen. Barbara Boxer wrote to the CIA director demanding an explanation. There were Senate hearings and three federal investigations on the topic. No evidence was found of any CIA effort to introduce crack cocaine to American communities.

In 1981, Washington, D.C., was convulsed by Gary Sick's allegations that the Reagan campaign had negotiated with the Iranian government to delay the release of American hostages until Reagan's inauguration. The House of Representatives and the Senate both investigated, as did several news organizations. The claim was found to be groundless.

In the 2000s, a number of left-wing entertainers along with assorted kooks such as Jesse Ventura and Alex Jones embraced the "9/11 truther" conspiracy—that the attacks were an inside job directed by George W. Bush.

This isn't to say that the right was free of the conspiracy cancer—more that it was in remission. Bill Buckley, who had reigned as the de facto leader of American conservatism for decades, excommunicated the John Birch Society, the anti-Semites and other conspiracy mongers of the right.

But in 2011, Donald Trump flamboyantly boosted the

"birther" conspiracy about Barack Obama in a "Today" show appearance. He claimed to have a team of investigators working in Hawaii, stating, "They cannot believe what they're finding." Trump was rewarded by moving to the top of Republicans' list of preferred presidential candidates for 2012. As to whether Trump actually ever sent anyone to Hawaii—that is open to doubt.

Historian Richard Hofstadter famously diagnosed the "paranoid style" of American politics. It's not clear that we suffer from paranoia more than others, but there is no doubt that conspiracy theories are inimical to social trust. The conspiracy theory about the CIA being responsible for the cocaine epidemic arguably did more damage to the spirits of people who believed their government capable of this than to the CIA itself.

President Trump's champions demand that so-called never-Trumpers acknowledge his accomplishments (which many do), yet they display no willingness to concede that they are paying a huge price in credibility by descending to truth-free tactics in defense of him.

Many conservative outlets are red-faced with indignation about a supposed conspiracy within the FBI and the "deep state" to destroy Donald Trump. The evidence? Justice Department officials may have relied, in part, on the "Democrat funded" Steele dossier to get a FISA warrant on Carter Page. A Republican FBI deputy director is married to a Democrat. An FBI agent (whom Robert Mueller fired) expressed dismay about Trump's election and joked with his mistress about a "secret society." This is partisan hysteria. Mueller will either find something or he won't. Attempting preemptively to discredit the investigation—which most Republicans initially welcomed—suggests lack of faith in their leader's innocence.

Trump has a promiscuous habit (no, not that one) of flinging wild accusations. The stable of enablers at Fox News, Breitbart and elsewhere who repeat his accusations of an FBI conspiracy cannot have forgotten so much so soon. In April 2016, after Ted Cruz won all the Colorado delegates, Trump fumed that the Republican Party was corrupt: "I'm hundreds of delegates ahead, but the system is rigged, folks. It's a rigged, disgusting dirty system. It's a dirty system, and only a nonpolitician would say it."

When the judge in the Trump University fraud case issued rulings Trump didn't care for, he declared that the judge was biased because of his ethnic background. He called the Indiana-born judge a "Mexican." (He settled the case after the election for $25 million.)

Anticipating a loss in 2016, Trump declined to vouch for the legitimacy of the coming vote. Later, haunted by losing the popular vote, he circulated baseless stories that millions of illegals voted in the 2016 election.

Conspiracy thinking is lazy, damaging and weak. It undermines the already shaky confidence Americans place in institutions. Trump revels in it. To see huge swaths of the Republican opinion elite following suit is acutely disappointing. Defend him if you choose, but don't become him.

Who Is Really Burning Things Down?

July 31, 2020

My friend David French, one of the most admirable voices in America today, argues that conservatives need not vote against Republican senate candidates in order to send a message about Trumpism. I disagree. He writes, "A rage, fury, and a 'burn it all down' mentality is one of the maladies that brought us to the present moment."

This assumes that the reason some plan to evict Republican senators is simply a matter of anger. But voting against a candidate or even a whole party is not nihilism. It's the legal, Constitutional way to express approval or disapproval. The current Republican Party has chosen to become the burn-it-all-down party. The most demoralizing aspect of the past four years has not been that a boob conman was elected president but that one of the two great political parties surrendered to him utterly.

David suggests that voting against Republican senators ignores that they had bad choices.

It's certainly true that Republicans perceived their options to be limited. If they speak up, they say, they will flush their careers down the drain. Look at what happened to Jeff Flake, Mark Sanford and Bob Corker!

But this overstates things. A number of Republicans have stood up to Trump and maintained their electoral viability—especially when they challenged him on matters in which he has shown little interest, namely public policy. Sen. Pat Toomey, R-Pa., for example, voted against the president's USMCA trade agreement and (gasp) wrote an op-ed in The Wall Street Journal explaining his reasoning.

When the president abruptly announced, following a phone

call with Turkish leader Recep Erdogan, that he was withdrawing American troops forthwith from Syria, a number of Republicans voiced horror. Sen. Ben Sasse, R-Neb., said it would lead to a "slaughter." Sen. Ted Cruz said it would be "DISGRACEFUL." Rep. Liz Cheney called it a "catastrophic mistake that puts our gains against ISIS at risk and threatens America's national security." Senators Lindsay Graham, R-S.C., Mitch McConnell, R-Ky., Mitt Romney, R-Utah, Marco Rubio, R-Fla., former U.N. Ambassador Nikki Haley and others weighed in as well.

When the president suggested lifting sanctions on Russia, Senator Rob Portman, R-Ohio, said it would be "horrible" for the United States. And after Gen. James Mattis wrote an op-ed saying that Donald Trump was making a "mockery of the U.S. Constitution," Sen. Lisa Murkowski said: "I was really thankful. I thought General Mattis' words were true, and honest and necessary and overdue."

So, it is possible to speak up about this president and survive. I use that word advisedly, because these Republican officeholders often use words like "kill" or "destroy" or "annihilate" when contemplating what Trump would do to them if they raise their heads too far above the parapet. In fact, all that actually threatened them was the possibility of nasty tweets and the chance that they might lose their seats.

David is right that very few people in any walk of life display courage on anything, though craven Republicans holding House and Senate posts might want to pause from time to time to contemplate the extraordinary valor of protesters in Hong Kong, Iran and Egypt who continue to put their freedom and sometimes their lives at risk by taking to the streets. And should being an elected official really be one's "life work"?

As noted above, Republicans have criticized the president on policy matters, sometimes even harshly. Where they have shrunk into their shells was on matters that are even more critical to the health of our republic. They have, by their silence, given assent to his cruelty, his assaults on truth, his dangerous flirtations with political violence and his consistent demolition of institutions.

Institutions are like scaffolding. When a society's institutions are weakened, the whole edifice can come crashing down.

Donald Trump undermined the institution of the free press, urging his followers to disbelieve everything except what came from the leader. He weakened respect for law enforcement and the courts, suggesting that he was the victim of a "deep state" and that "so-called judges" need not be respected. He scorned allies and toadied to dictators. He has cast doubt on the integrity of elections. He ran the executive branch like a gangster, demanding personal loyalty and abusing officials such as the hapless Jeff Sessions, who merely followed ethics rules. He ignored the law to get his way on the border wall. He violated the most sacred norms of a multiethnic society by encouraging racial hatred. He made the U.S. guilty of separating babies from their mothers.

Elected officials, terrified of their own constituents, have cowered and temporized in the face of a truly unprecedented assault on democratic values. They believed that they were powerless and acted accordingly. Since they were powerless when it counted, perhaps we should make it official?

Quazy for QAnon

Aug. 14, 2020

"I can no longer sit back and allow Communist infiltration … to sap and impurify all of our precious bodily fluids."—Air Force Brigadier General Jack D. Ripper, "Dr. Strangelove"

In the 1964 black comedy "Dr. Strangelove," the above words are spoken by a general who is about to start World War III. His theory about the contamination of "precious bodily fluids" is the tipoff for poor Group Captain Lionel Mandrake that the general has gone certifiably cuckoo.

This week, Republican voters in Georgia's 14th congressional district nominated Marjorie Taylor Greene for the seat being vacated by Rep. Tom Graves. Greene is (or claims to be) a QAnon believer.

You might think that once voters were alerted to this, they'd shrink from Greene as Mandrake did from Ripper, asking her to go nicely with the men in white coats who are here to help her. Her opponent told Politico, "She is not conservative—she's crazy." The voters were not convinced. Greene trounced Cowan by 14 points (as of this writing).

Georgia 14 is a comfortably Republican district. But Greene is not offering traditional Republican fare. She's denounced a "Muslim invasion" of America, called George Soros a "Nazi," and endorsed the bonkers QAnon conspiracy.

Q refers to an Energy Department classification level of top secret. The person styling himself Q in cryptic online messages is anonymous, thus QAnon. To describe what followers of Q believe is to enter a hall of mirrors.

Remember the fellow who, a month after the 2016 election, drove from North Carolina to D.C., barging into a pizza place and firing off a shotgun? Well, he was looking for the child sex slaves he'd been led to believe were chained in the back, at the behest of John Podesta and Hillary Clinton.

"Pizzagate" morphed into the QAnon conspiracy in which Q followers wait for signals from their leader that a vast conspiracy of Satanic child abusers, run by the "deep state," George Soros, the Supreme Court and God knows who else is about to be unmasked. Did I mention that they think Beyonce is only pretending to be black? It's a hydra-headed thing, this conspiracy, and contains multitudes. But the one common thread is this: The great deliverer will be Donald J. Trump.

The internet age has birthed a crisis of information. Flooded by claims and counterclaims, people don't know whom to trust. And in this welter of confusion, many seize upon stories they'd like to be true, rather than those that seem plausible. I guess it's more comforting for some to believe that Trump's erratic and incompetent behavior is actually cover for a massive plan to save the world from Satan-worshipping child molesters than to accept that he is what he seems.

People carrying Q signs began showing up at Trump rallies in 2018. The phrases "Calm Before the Storm" and "Where We Go One, We Go All" have become talismanic. Trump has done nothing to discourage the cult. On the contrary, he posed in the Oval Office with Michael Lebron, a Q promoter. Trump's former national security advisor, Michael Flynn, believed to be the eponymous Q by several adherents, has signaled to Q followers in a video release. He follows a recitation of the oath of office for federal officials with the line "Where We Go One, We Go All." (My guess is that Flynn is in it for the cash.)

No fewer than 60 current or former congressional candidates have expressed interest in or support for the QAnon conspiracy. One of them, Jo Rae Perkins, got the Republican nomination for Senate in Oregon. And now Marjorie Taylor Greene seems almost certain to be going to Congress.

Greene claimed that the Republican "establishment" was against her. But alas, that's not true. House Minority Whip Steve

Scalise and GOP Conference Chair Liz Cheney did condemn her remarks. But Greene received backing from the House Freedom Fund, an arm of the House Freedom Caucus. Rep. Jim Jordan of Ohio and former Rep. Mark Meadows, now Trump's chief of staff, also backed Greene. Trump himself has cheered her election and called her a future Republican star.

Most Americans have not heard of QAnon. But the paranoid conspiracy has gathered momentum at the Republican grassroots. The taste for crazy seems peculiarly partisan. When Democrats go off the deep end, it tends to be for Marxism or Maoism. Those are among the most dangerous political ideas in the world and have led directly to the deaths of scores of millions of people. But they're not nuts.

It's odd that Republicans, who pride themselves on their practical understanding of life—incentives matter, money doesn't grow on trees, personal responsibility is essential to a well-ordered society—should display such a marked weakness for utter lunacy. I don't offer an explanation, just a warning. This disordered thinking is no longer just a fringe phenomenon. Unlike Group Captain Mandrake, a lot of Republicans out there don't recognize crazy when they see it.

Flight 93 Forever

Sept. 18, 2020

Danielle Pletka, senior fellow at the American Enterprise Institute, has announced that while she never considered voting for Donald Trump in 2016, she may well do so this year. She is being driven to this extremity, she says, by the "hard left ideologues" of the Democratic Party.

Judging by chatter on the right, this rationalization—so redolent of the Flight 93 argument from 2016—is somewhat popular. So, let's take a closer look.

Though she dutifully wrist slaps Trump for his lies and tweets, she does so as a backhanded compliment. The trouble with his style is that it "has managed to obscure his administration's more-substantive accomplishments, such as focusing the world's attention on China's threat to global security and brokering a new era of Middle East peace." So, you see, it's not that he is degrading the very idea of truth or undermining cherished national ideals, it's just that those darned tweets distract from his great accomplishments!

The notion that Trump has awakened the world to the threat from China is risible. He has, in fact, been played by China. After four years of tariffs and obsequiousness toward Xi Jinping, China is more powerful and the U.S. weaker. Trump may deserve a measure of credit for the peace deals between Israel and the Gulf Arab states, but it's more likely that those are the unintended consequences of Obama's Iran deal, which scared the Gulf States into Israel's arms.

But her chief complaint is not about foreign affairs. "Joe Biden would be a figurehead president, incapable of focus or leadership, who would run a teleprompter presidency with the words drafted by his party's hard-left ideologues."

What is the evidence for this? Biden ran a centrist campaign throughout the Democratic primaries despite lots of encouragement to tilt left. He resisted the siren song of "Medicare for All," and opposed open borders, free public college tuition, banning fracking and defunding the police. If the left couldn't budge him when he was just one candidate in a field of 29, what makes people think they will have better luck when he is the party's nominee—or the president of the United States?

Besides, these congeries of horrors assume that if Democrats achieve majorities in both houses and take the White House in 2020, the democratic process will be over. The pedestrian truth is that if Democrats overestimate their mandate and go too far, they may find that voters clip their wings in 2022. Amazing how that works.

What these doomsday scenarios also overlook is that if Biden is elected and Democrats take the Senate, they are going to have their hands full attempting to guide the nation safely through the remainder of this pandemic.

But perhaps Pletka only gets to her true complaint toward the end:

"I fear the grip of Manhattan-San Francisco progressive mores ... (and) virtue-signaling bullies who increasingly try to ... encourage my children to think that their being White is intrinsically evil ... and the leftist vigilantes who view every personal choice—from recipes to hairdos—through their twisted prisms of politics and culture."

If Pletka is genuinely alarmed by the extremism of the left, maybe the best solution is not to throw herself into the arms of an openly racist, authoritarian right-wing extremist who embodies every stereotype the left harbors about conservatives. Pletka doesn't like Manhattan-San Francisco progressivism. Neither do I. But like so many in modern America, she confuses cultural and political arguments. We don't elect a chief executive to outlaw drag queen story hour.

Nor does the left operate in a vacuum. The extremism of the

right, enthroned in the White House no less, is stimulating ever more reaction from the left.

Pletka highlights this or that sin or tendency on the part of "progressives" and declares it to be the true essence of the Democratic Party. Meanwhile, she disregards Trump and the grotesque menagerie he has invited into public life.

People on the left and in the center would be forgiven for concluding that Trump is precisely the "mainstream of the Republican Party" if he is reelected. And who among the leaders of the Democratic Party has offered anything like the encouragement to extremism that Trump has given to QAnon and the vigilantes on the streets?

The one essential rock upon which this country depends is the rule of law. It's more crucial than blocking "Medicare for All," more essential even than preventing another Iran nuclear deal. If the rule of law is undermined as Trump is doing and threatens to accelerate, everything else—prosperity, civil cohesion, security—is in danger. Those are the stakes, not the filibuster, not hairstyles and not virtue signaling.

McConnell Condemns QAnon, Except When He Doesn't

Feb. 4, 2021

So, *now* Mitch McConnell tells us that Marjorie Taylor Greene's views are a "cancer" on the Republican Party and on the country. Odd that he neglected to make that point when one of his preferred candidates in the Georgia runoff, Kelly Loeffler, campaigned with Greene.

McConnell is now leaning heavily on the other body to clean up its act, denouncing "looney lies and conspiracy theories." McConnell's deputy in Senate leadership, John Thune, chimed in, too, asking his colleagues: "Do they want to be the party of limited government … free markets, peace through strength and pro-life, or do they want to be the party of conspiracy theories and QAnon?"

The party's dilemma, we're told, is captured by two members of Congress. On the one hand, you have Liz Cheney, three term, at-large representative from Wyoming and the third-ranking Republican in the House. A former deputy assistant secretary of state, she is known for her interest in national security, child protection and, until the attack on the Capitol, reliable support for Donald Trump.

Cheney is getting blowback within the party because she voted to impeach Trump after the attack on Congress. The Wyoming GOP put out a statement calling Cheney's vote to hold Trump accountable for the worst sedition in 160 years a "travesty." The execrable Matt Gaetz flew from his home district in the Florida panhandle to Cheyenne to hold a rally against her, which featured a phone-in from Donald Trump Jr. And at least 107 House Republicans have indicated that they would vote to oust Cheney from her leadership role in a secret ballot. A Wall Street Journal editorial characterized this as a "few dozen backbenchers," but it's actually an outright majority of the caucus.

And then, on the other hand, we have Marjorie Taylor Greene, representative of all that is insane in America. She believes that the Parkland shootings were staged, that QAnon is right about the pedophilic cannibals populating the Democratic Party, that Nancy Pelosi should be murdered, that Donald Trump won the 2020 election and that Jewish space lasers caused the California wildfires last year. (You don't think fires start themselves, do you?) Her Republican primary opponent, Dr. John Cowan, described her this way: "I'm a neurosurgeon. I diagnose crazy every day. It took five minutes talking to her to realize there were bats in the attic."

Weighing Cheney against Greene, the Republican Party is dithering. In responding to demands that the party strip Greene of her committee assignments as they did to Steve King, Andy Biggs of the ironically named "Freedom Caucus" fumed: "The Democrats' moves to strip Congresswoman Greene of her committee assignments for thoughts and opinions she shared as a private citizen before coming to the U.S. House is unprecedented and unconstitutional. ... Republicans, beware: If this can happen to Congresswoman Marjorie Taylor Greene, it can happen to any one of us."

Well, there you have it—the perfect path to discrediting all Republicans. Biggs, Gaetz, Jim Jordan and others are throwing their arms around Greene and confirming that her crazed rantings are indistinguishable from other Republicans. Fox host Tucker Carlson made a similar case recently when he mocked those who warn of Greene's vicious, contemptible conspiracy-mongering:

"This new member of Congress has barely even voted ... But CNN says she has bad opinions. ... Now if you're skeptical about any of this, our advice is keep it to yourself. Because free inquiry is dead, unauthorized questions are hate speech."

Welcome to anti-anti-QAnon. "Free inquiry is dead," proclaims Carlson to an estimated 5 million viewers. We have reached the farcical moment when even to criticize a tinfoil-hat conspiracist is denounced as "silencing." No one is fining or jailing Greene for her opinions. To deny her a seat on the House Education and Labor Committee is not exactly the Gulag.

Look, it's great that a number of Senate Republicans are speaking forcefully about quarantining QAnonism. Todd Young was refreshingly frank:

"The people of her congressional district, it's their prerogative if they want to abase themselves by voting to elect someone who indulges in anti-Semitic conspiracy theories and all manner of other nonsense. But I've got no tolerance for people like that. In terms of the divisions within our party, she's not even part of the conversation, as far as I'm concerned."

But these senators might want to consider the elephant in the room. Who phoned Marjorie Taylor Greene to express support after her "Rothschild space laser" comments became public? Who called her a "rising star" of the GOP? Who said QAnon people "love their country"? And who is it that all of the aforementioned senators seem poised to acquit again?

Greene is the easy target for these newly fastidious Republicans. They opened the tent long ago to the villains, liars, and conspiracists when they welcomed the ringmaster. With one side of their mouths, they denounce the looney haters, but with the other, they seize a fig leaf to disguise their fear of convicting Trump. If they want to cleanse the Republican Party of the poisons that are rapidly killing it, they can vote to hold the man who first infected it with QAnon, "election fraud" and much more, accountable. That, not restraining Greene, is the lustration the party needs.

The Party of Violence

Sept. 3, 2021

 A Republican running for Northampton County executive in Pennsylvania gave a heated address on Aug. 29 about mask mandates in schools. Steve Lynch is tired, he said, of providing his school board arguments and data (he apparently thinks the data support letting kids go maskless), but the important thing about his rant is the threat of force: "Forget into these school boards with frigging data. ... They don't follow the law! You go in and you remove 'em. I'm going in there with 20 strong men."

 That's the kind of language that Republicans are now employing. Lynch has not run for public office before, but he did attend the Jan. 6 rally in Washington, D.C., and has posted on social media that the violence that day was a false-flag operation meant to discredit Trump supporters.

 Rep. Madison Cawthorn of North Carolina spoke last weekend at an event sponsored by the Macon County Republican Party. He delivered the kind of lies that have become routine among some Republicans. The election was stolen—and not just the presidential contest but also that won by Gov. Roy Cooper (who defeated his opponent by a quarter of a million votes). Cawthorn told the crowd that vaccines are harmful to children and urged them to "defend their children." A woman asked what he plans to do about the "535 Americans who have been captured from Jan, 6." Cawthorn, who has apparently heard this before, thundered, "Political hostages!" When someone in the crowd asked, "When are you gonna call us back to Washington?" he replied, "We are actively working on that one."

 Insurrection talk is becoming Cawthorn's specialty: "If our election systems continue to be rigged and continue to be stolen, then it's going to lead to one place—and it's bloodshed."

Naturally, former President Donald Trump has endorsed him for "whatever he wants to do."

In neighboring Tennessee, the Williamson County school board was disrupted by anti-mask parents. As doctors and nurses testified that masks would help limit the spread of COVID-19, people cursed and threatened them: "We will find you!" "We know who you are!"

In Georgia, a mobile vaccination site had to be shut down after anti-vaccine protesters showed up to threaten and harass health care workers. "Aside from feeling threatened themselves, staff realized no one would want to come to that location for a vaccination under those circumstances, so they packed up and left," a spokeswoman for the state health department told the Atlanta Journal Constitution.

A survey of the rest of the country yields yet more examples.

We are all old enough to remember a time when election workers were public-spirited citizens, usually elderly, who volunteered their time (or got very modest compensation) to sit for hours at polling sites scanning names from lists of voters and handing out little stickers. That America is gone, driven out by a radicalized Republican party. A number of states with Republican majorities have passed laws that would impose criminal fines of up to $25,000 for "offenses" such as permitting a ballot drop box to be accessible before early voting hours or sending an unsolicited absentee ballot application to a voter.

But that's not the worst of it. Election workers have been hounded and threatened. Bomb threats have been emailed to election sites. "You and your family will be killed very slowly," read a text message sent to Tricia Raffensperger after her husband, Georgia Secretary of State Brad Raffensperger, declined to "find" enough votes to flip the state to Trump. As many as 1 in 3 election workers has reported feeling unsafe, and thousands are resigning.

When Rep. Liz Cheney made the principled decision to vote for Trump's impeachment, she noted that one reason more

Republicans might not have chosen to join her was that "there were members who told me that they were afraid for their own security—afraid, in some instances, for their lives."

Republicans talk incessantly about other people's violence. The rioters who burned buildings after George Floyd's death. The criminals who make Chicago a murder capital. Immigrants who supposedly terrorize their host nation (they don't).

Criminal violence is a problem, but the kind of violence Republicans are now flirting with or sometimes outright endorsing is political—and therefore on a completely different plane of threat.

Kyle Rittenhouse, an ill-supervised teenager who decided to grab an AR-15 and shoot people at a Kenosha, Wisconsin, riot (killing two and wounding one) was lionized by the GOP. His mother got a standing ovation at a fundraiser in Waukesha. Ashli Babbitt has become a martyr. Allen West, former chair of the Texas GOP, speaks approvingly of secession. Former National Security Adviser and Trump confidant Michael Flynn suggests that we need a Myanmar-style coup. Some 28% of Republicans respond affirmatively to the proposition that "because things have gotten so far off track" in the U.S., "true American patriots may have to resort to violence" to save the country.

Maybe that's not so bad? Not even a third. Another poll framed it differently: "The traditional American way of life is disappearing so fast that we may have to use force to save it." Fifty-six percent of Republicans agreed.

They are playing with fire. Nothing less than democratic legitimacy is on the line. These menacing signals suggest that Jan. 6 may have been the overture, not the finale.

How to Disarm the Crazies

April 15, 2022

There is probably no easy cure for the Marjorie Taylor Greene phenomenon. She's a repellent clown whose presence on the national stage has yielded nothing but degradation—except for the guffaw she afforded us when denouncing Nancy Pelosi's "Gazpacho police."

And she has lots of company. Her colleagues in the House include Paul Gosar and Matt Gaetz and Lauren Boebert and Louie Gohmert and, sigh, many more. And even among the members who probably do know the difference between the Nazi secret police and a summer soup, there are alarming numbers who are extremist-adjacent. There are, for example, more sitting GOP congressmen who voted not to certify the 2020 election than there are Republicans who voted for a resolution to support NATO.

Democrats are not immune to the extremism virus either. While the Democratic Party hasn't lost its bearings in the way the Republican Party has, it is skewed by its own zealots. In the 2020 presidential primaries, for example, progressive activists pushed candidates to impose a moratorium on deportations, to abolish private health insurance and to ban fracking, among other demands. Those issues weren't top of mind for average Democrats, let alone for average voters.

In the pre-internet era, our stable political parties seemed to be bulwarks of stability. But that has long since ceased to be the case. Rather than forming, directing and disciplining their members, these institutions have become hollow shells. Unable to control fundraising due to the rise of small-dollar, internet contributions, and stripped even of the formerly coveted power of attaching earmarks to legislation, the parties, as Yuval Levin has argued, are mere soapboxes that permit members to flaunt their personal brands.

The party duopoly empowers the most extreme voters and leaves the vast middle unrepresented and feeling that in general elections they must choose the lesser of two evils. As Katherine Gehl, founder of the Institute for Political Innovation, notes, about 10% of voters (those who vote in primaries) determine the outcome of 83% of congressional races. And because primary voters tend to be more ideological and extreme than others, candidates pander to them to get elected and then to remain in office. The term "primary" became a verb only in the last decade or so, as the power of the party zealots became a cudgel to use against any member who even considered compromising with the other party.

There's one more factor aggravating the lurch to extremism, at least among Republicans (Democrats have different rules), and that's the winner-take-all system in presidential primaries. In 2016, Donald Trump lost Iowa and then won New Hampshire with 35% of the vote. A solid majority, 57%, was divided among five other candidates.

So, are we doomed to be at the mercy of the mad and bad? It's possible, but then again, one reform that seems to be getting traction is ranked-choice voting (also known as instant runoff elections).

It's already the law in Alaska and Maine for state, congressional and presidential contests and has been adopted by more than 20 cities. In Virginia, the Republican Party used a ranked-choice system to choose its gubernatorial candidate in 2021, with the result that Glenn Youngkin rather than Amanda Chase ("Trump in heels") secured the nomination. In New York City, predictions that the city's 5.6 million voters would find the ranked-choice system confusing were not borne out. Turnout was up compared with the last contested mayoral primary, and 95% of voters said the system was easy. There were no differences among ethnic groups in understanding the system, and the winner was a moderate former cop.

There are many different approaches to ranked-choice voting, and experimentation will determine which is best. But even with the small sample we have, we can judge that the incentives seem better. Among the three GOP senators who voted to confirm Ketanji Brown Jackson to the Supreme Court, only one is up for reelection in 2022—Lisa Murkowski of Alaska. Murkowski could uphold the norm of confirming the other party's qualified nominee and not fear a Trumpist primary challenger because Alaska now holds an open primary in which anyone from any party can participate. The four candidates who win the most votes go on to the general election. Voters rank their choices. If one candidate gets over 50%, he or she is the winner. If not, the bottom polling candidate is dropped, and the second choices on ballots are distributed, and so on until someone has a majority.

Not only does the ranked-choice system disempower party extremists; it also discourages candidates from savage personal attacks, the persistence of which arguably keeps some fine people out of politics altogether.

The two-party system has not proven to be a solid foundation for democracy. Time to disarm the crazies.

Republicans Are Rooting for Civil War

Aug. 12, 2022

Executing a valid search warrant, FBI agents arrived in the morning to search the office. The word "unprecedented" was on everyone's lips. They seized business records, computers and other documents related to possible crimes. An enraged Donald Trump denounced the FBI and the Justice Department, saying not that they had abided by the warrant issued by a federal judge, but rather that agents had "broken into" the office.

The year was 2018, and Trump was livid about the FBI's investigation into his longtime attorney/fixer, Michael Cohen.

At the time, many observers, including me, assumed that the investigation would yield bushels of incriminating documents about Trump. Cohen was his personal lawyer, after all, the guy who wrote the hush-money checks to porn stars and presumably had access to many of Trump's dodgy or downright illegal acts. It didn't turn out that way.

But what is not open to doubt is that the Republican Party, which seemed to be flirting with post-Trumpism just a few weeks ago, has now come roaring back as an authoritarian cult. Trump has not changed. But he has changed Republicans.

Consider 2018 again. When the FBI searched Cohen's office, Trump was Trump. He raged like a banshee. He declared that it was "an attack on our country" and a "disgraceful situation."

Some Fox News bobbleheads treated the story as more evidence of a conspiracy to hurt the Dear Leader, but most Republicans were subdued. The prevailing tone in Republican ranks was that the investigations, including Robert Mueller's, must be permitted to proceed according to the rules. Sens. Thom Tillis and Lindsey Graham, for example, teamed up with their

Democratic colleagues, Sens. Chris Coons and Cory Booker, to propose the Special Counsel Independence and Integrity Act.

Four years later, the FBI has executed another warrant, this time to Trump's office, and the Trump forces have gone berserk. Rep. Paul Gosar tweeted, "I will support a complete dismantling and elimination of the democrat brown shirts known as the FBI. This is too much for our republic to withstand ..."

Anthony Sabatini, a Florida state representative and candidate for Congress, was prepared to dismantle the whole federalist structure: "It's time for us in the Florida Legislature to ... sever all ties with DOJ immediately. Any FBI agent conducting law enforcement functions outside the purview of our State should be arrested upon sight." That would go well.

Sen. Josh Hawley tweeted that "At a minimum, Garland must resign or be impeached. The search warrant must be published. (FBI Director) Christopher Wray must be removed. And the FBI reformed top to bottom."

Rep. Marjorie Taylor Greene chants, "Defund the FBI."

Newt Gingrich suggests that the feds might have planted evidence at Mar-a-Lago.

The party that backed the blue and disdained the defund-the-police crowd now flips. Gingrich is channeling Johnnie Cochran. Trump may be an ignoramus and a clod, but he has the capacity to turn people inside out.

Rep. Kevin McCarthy, the likely next speaker of the House, tweeted a threat to the attorney general, telling Garland to "preserve your documents and clear your calendar" because when/if Republicans take the majority, they're coming for him.

Now, as a substantive matter, McCarthy's tweet is meaningless. The House of Representatives, along with the Senate, already exercises oversight authority over the Justice Department. But the importance of the tweet is not its substance but its tone—the call for vengeance. McCarthy displays zero interest in whether Trump actually committed a crime. The clear message is, "You've gone after our leader, so we're coming for you." The merits of Garland's actions are irrelevant. The facts are irrelevant. It's war.

For some in the wooly precincts of the MAGA right, the call to arms was literal. As Vice reported, some Trumpists were explicit: "'Civil War 2.0 just kicked off,' one user wrote on Twitter, with another adding, 'One step closer to a kinetic civil war.' Others said they were ready to take part: 'I already bought my ammo.'" Steve Bannon, who was pardoned for bilking Trump supporters who thought they were building a wall, declared that "we're at war" and called the FBI the "Gestapo."

Trump is a sick soul who cannot imagine a world in which people act on principle or think about the welfare of others. While in power, Trump wanted to use the FBI to punish his political opponents ("Lock her up") and reward his friends ("Go easy on Michael Flynn"). He projects his own corrupt motives onto others and assumes that the FBI investigation is nothing but a Democratic power grab. It would be pathetic if he had not dragged an entire political party into the fever swamps with him.

This experiment in self-government requires a minimum amount of social trust to succeed. With every tweet that spreads cynicism and lies; with every call to arms that welcomes civil conflict; Trumpist Republicans are poisoning the nation they claim so ostentatiously to love.

What Country Is the Wall Street Journal Living in?

Sept. 30, 2022

The headline of a Wall Street Journal editorial caught my eye: "Arizona's School Choice Election." Writing as if nothing had changed in American politics since 2011, the editorial board assailed Katie Hobbs, the Democratic candidate for governor, as a tool of the teachers unions for her opposition to school choice. The Journal advised that parents would be well-advised to vote Republican.

There you have it: the failure of the intellectual leaders of conservatism in one editorial. The once magisterial voice of the conservative worldview looked at the race for governor in Arizona and airily overlooked reality. School choice? Are they out of their minds?

Disturbing, extremist and otherwise unfit candidates dot the national landscape in 2022 like monkeypox, from Doug Mastriano in Pennsylvania to J.D. Vance in Ohio to Don Bolduc in New Hampshire, but Arizona surely takes the highest honors for the sheer concentration of ranting incompetents who threaten the democratic process.

Kari Lake, the Republican candidate for governor, whom the Journal is endorsing, may be in favor of school choice, but that's a little beside the point when you consider the larger picture. Lake has declared that the 2020 election was "corrupt and stolen." Regarding the current president of the United States, she has expressed pity, urging that "Deep down, I think we all know this illegitimate fool in the White House—I feel sorry for him—didn't win. I hope Americans are smart enough to know that." She has no patience for temporizers. "It is not enough to say you are for

'Election Integrity' if you are not for DECERTIFYING the 2020 election if wrongdoing, fraud or different results are revealed," she tweeted last year.

There is no fiction she has not willingly endorsed. She told a group of young women that they shouldn't take precautions about COVID because "The truth is that hydroxychloroquine works and other inexpensive treatments work." A week before the voting, she announced, "We're already detecting some stealing going on." And despite her victory, she carried a sledgehammer onstage on primary night and pantomimed smashing electronic voting machines.

That's the GOP nominee for governor of Arizona. What does The Wall Street Journal do with these awkward realities? The board interprets them as problems *only insofar as they make it harder for her to win*.

"GOP gubernatorial nominee Kari Lake hasn't helped herself or her party by insisting that the 2020 election was stolen. Her election fraud claims put off many Republicans and independents and are a loser in the general election. A winning and unifying issue for Republicans this November is school choice."

The important thing is for the election-denying cult member to win, so let's find something that can distract disaffected Republicans and independents.

Despite all of the foregoing, it's just possible that Lake is the most mainstream of the major Republican candidates in Arizona this year. The GOP nominee for Senate is Blake Masters, an election denier who spices up the usual fare with great replacement talk. "The Democrats dream of mass amnesty, because they want to import a new electorate," he says. He attributes America's problems with gun violence to "Black people, frankly." When asked for a "subversive" thinker he admires, he responded with "How about, like, Theodore Kaczynski?" Yes, Wall Street Journal editorial board, how about that?

But wait, we're not finished with Arizona's contributions to national insanity. The Republican candidate for secretary of state in Arizona is not just an election-denying extremist enemy of democracy, but a card-carrying member of the Oath Keepers, the fine gentlemen who are currently being tried in federal court for seditious conspiracy. Mark Finchem has appeared on QAnon-linked radio talk shows and spoke at a rally in January with Trump, Mike Lindell and the whole clown car of kooks. His website features a banner inviting readers to "Sign the petition to decertify and set aside AZ electors." Soon he may be the secretary of state of Arizona.

Some are able to see what is at stake here. When Liz Cheney was asked whether she might campaign for Democrat Katie Hobbs, she said yes. "In this election, you have to vote for the person who actually believes in democracy."

Again, I tend to agree with the Journal's editorial board on many policy matters. But they are pretending, or perhaps deluding themselves, that the Republican Party remains, underneath it all, the party of Paul Ryan and Larry Hogan and Chris Sununu, and that the country will be better off if Republicans win elections, full stop.

But as Liz Cheney sees and is willing to say, not this Republican Party. This GOP is the party of Mastriano and Vance and, yes, Kari Lake. This is a party that cannot be trusted with power; that openly proclaims its eagerness to overturn elections. Next to that, everything else, including school choice and regulation and taxes, pales to insignificance. The Wall Street Journal editorial board has continuing influence with reasonable center-right voters. They owe them better.

Why Are You a Patriot?

Oct. 21, 2022

A few months ago, some marketer got hold of my cellphone number, and I've been deluged ever since with text appeals from MAGA world and the GOP. One sample from just the last few days:

"IMPEACH BIDEN POLL DUE TONIGHT! Mona, we're begging, please take 30 seconds to join fellow patriots and take the official GOP poll."

Watching the midterms play out, and seeing the GOP nominate people like Herschel Walker, Don Bolduc, Doug Mastriano and Kari Lake, I am struck by a strange incongruity. The MAGA messages incessantly invoke love of America. But it's worth pausing to wonder what they love.

Their professed love for America leads them to rally around Walker, who seems to be both a mentally unstable and bad man. It's not just run-of-the-mill lies such as claiming that he graduated in the top 1% of his class at the University of Georgia when in truth he didn't graduate at all. Those lies are bad, but differ in degree more than kind from exaggerations we've heard from politicians in the past.

No, the more pernicious lies are the ones that bring actual virtues into disrepute. Walker has made promoting responsible fatherhood part of his image. He has gone even further (perhaps in an effort to score points among white conservatives) by calling out irresponsible Black fathers in particular. In a 2021 interview he said: "If you have a child with a woman, even if you have to leave that woman … you don't leave that child." And speaking to Charlie Kirk, he boasted that he had served as a father figure for young African American kids in his hometown of Wrightsville,

Georgia, but that he should have done more. "I want to apologize to the African American community, because the fatherless home is a major, major problem."

So when the Daily Beast revealed that Walker had not one, not two, but three unacknowledged children he had not raised, and that this advocate for "no exceptions" to laws outlawing abortion had paid for one abortion and encouraged another, it all might have been too much for a party that had even a nodding familiarity with integrity. But no, Sens. Rick Scott and Tom Cotton, Republican National Committee chair Ronna (used to be Romney) McDaniel, and Ralph Reed of the Faith and Freedom Coalition rallied behind Walker.

Now, hypocrisy is the tribute that vice pays to virtue, but if you're caught in hypocrisy, you have to take the consequences, otherwise people could get the idea that you are total cynics who don't really believe in anything except power.

And this brings us back to patriotism because one of the reasons to love your country is that it elevates certain virtues like integrity, courage, decency and honor. Politics is a tough business that frequently attracts ambitious, less-than-sterling people. But surely one aspect of patriotism is revulsion at seeing your nation's leadership sullied by flagrant liars, bigots and cheats. You don't want to elevate someone who sent buses to the Capitol on Jan. 6 and consorts with antisemites, or who admires the Unabomber, or who believes that "Mike Pence is a traitor," or who questions the legitimacy of our elections as a majority of GOP nominees this year do. Yet those are the leaders who get GOP pulses racing.

Another aspect of this faux patriotism is the attraction to autocrats and thugs around the globe. While it's true that America doesn't have an unblemished record when it comes to international affairs (who does?), one of the things that always nurtured my own patriotic sentiment was the overall sense that we were the good guys—or at least tried to be. Of course we did business with bad regimes and had friendly relations with some very dubious allies (like Saudi Arabia), but we were also the lifeline for struggling democracies like Taiwan, Israel and South Korea. When the world faces an emergency like a tsunami or a famine or an act of raw aggression, they don't phone Xi or Putin; they call the White House.

But the GOP today, while draping itself in the mantle of patriotism, is signaling that in the greatest challenge to freedom in the globe today—the unprovoked, imperialist, brutal invasion of Ukraine by Russia—they are seriously considering cutting off aid to Ukraine.

Minority Leader and would-be House Speaker Kevin McCarthy is saying that a Republican-majority Congress would not "write a blank check" to Ukraine. With their courage and sacrifice, they are redeeming the idea of liberty at a time when many around the world were losing faith in democracy. Ukrainians are demonstrating that, contrary to the propaganda of autocrats everywhere, democracies are actually stronger than dictatorships. And they are showing that some things, like the right to live free—to think what you want, read what you want, worship as you wish and say what you think—are worth fighting and dying for.

The America I love is wholeheartedly behind Ukraine. McCarthy and big swaths of his party claim to love America, but they make this nation less worthy of patriotism.

The Right Needs Hunter Biden

Dec. 9, 2022

The right is positively giddy over the so-called Twitter files. House Republicans called a press conference to declare that their very top priority will be investigating Hunter Biden's laptop. Rep. Elise Stefanik promised in July that if given the majority, Republicans would get "accountability" from the "Biden crime family." The victim narrative—that big Tech rigged the 2020 election by suppressing the Hunter laptop story—is all the rage on the right.

"We're learning in real-time how Twitter colluded to silence the truth about Hunter Biden's laptop just days before the 2020 presidential election," Rep. Kevin McCarthy tweeted, and the whole right-wing chorus has sung along. They haven't been this energized since the FBI executed a search warrant at Mar-a-Lago. Laura Ingraham cheered Elon Musk on for uncovering the "fact" that Twitter "worked overtime" to elect Biden. Republican National Committee Chair Ronna Romney McDaniel offered that "If Joe Biden were a Republican, this would be getting nonstop coverage by the mainstream media. Their blatant bias would be unbelievable except it happens EVERY SINGLE TIME." Self-described "psychedelic adventurer" Joe Rogan suggests that this proves that "The deep state is 100% real. The swamp is real. They're real monsters, and they were really trying to get rid of him (Trump) by lying."

The notion that a laptop delivered to the Post by Rudy Giuliani two weeks before the election and rejected by The New York Times, The Wall Street Journal, Fox News and others should *not* have been treated skeptically is the dicier proposition. Further, the hyperventilating about the assault this represents on the First Amendment is risible. Twitter, a private company, was free to ignore the request. Even if Biden had been president at the time, there would be no violation of the First Amendment. Government officials not infrequently request that journalists refrain from publishing material, often about military secrets. Newspapers sometimes comply and sometimes not. It's only a violation of the First Amendment if the government coerces the journalists.

Nor did Twitter's temporary suspension of the Post's account sway the election. As Cathy Young notes, 1) the ban lasted only about 36 hours; 2) the ban may have heightened interest in the story rather than suppressing it, and in any case, the story was available via a Google search; and 3) the whole narrative about Biden's participation in Ukrainian corruption, the gravamen of the laptop story, is false.

So what is this really about? Consider the timing.

For seven years, the right has been explaining, excusing, avoiding and eventually cheering the most morally depraved figure in American politics. That takes a toll on the psyche. You can tell yourself that the critics are unhinged, suffering from "Trump derangement syndrome," but then Trump will do what he always does—make a fool of you. You denied that Trump purposely broke the law when he took highly classified documents to Mar-a-Lago and obstructed every effort to retrieve them. And then what does Trump do? He admits taking them! You scoff at the critics who've compared Trump with Nazis. And then what does he do? He has dinner with Nazis! (And fails to condemn them even after the fact.) You despised people who claimed Trump was a threat to the Constitution, and then Trump explicitly calls for "terminating" the Constitution in order to put himself back in the Oval Office.

Hunter Biden seems to be a mess. But there is nothing relevant to public policy or civic virtue here. Joe Biden is hardly the first president to have troubled family members. But Joe Biden didn't hire Hunter at the White House, and if there is any evidence of the president using official influence on Hunter's behalf, we haven't seen it. The Department of Justice under Trump opened an investigation into Hunter Biden. President Biden has left it alone. It's ongoing.

The right has a deep psychological need for the Hunter Biden story. They desperately want Joe Biden to be corrupt and for the whole family to be, in Stefanik's words, "a crime family" because they have provided succor and support to someone who has encouraged political violence since his early rallies in 2015, has stoked hatred of minorities through lies, has used his office for personal gain in the most flagrant fashion, has surrounded himself with criminals and con men, has committed human rights violations against would-be immigrants by separating children from their parents, has pardoned war criminals, has cost the lives of tens of thousands of COVID patients by discounting the virus and peddling quack cures, has revived racism in public discourse, and has attempted a violent coup d'etat.

They know it. But here's something else they need to meditate on: Even if everything they're alleging about Joe Biden were true; even if he did pull strings to help his son and even profited unjustly thereby, it still wouldn't amount to a fraction of what Trump did. And it still won't wash out the "damn'd spot."

The Normalization of Marjorie Taylor Greene

Jan. 13, 2023

During one of Kevin McCarthy's gauntlet of punishing votes, it was striking to see with whom he passed the time. There she was, dressed in sophisticated black, the member hailed as a "key ally" to the new speaker of the House: Marjorie Taylor Greene.

Her choice of color (in the past she has donned stark reds, whites or blues—get it?) is perhaps a signal of the new Greene—a mainstream figure, a serious politician. Her status was signaled by a respectful, not to say softball interview with Howard Kurtz on Fox News.

Doubtless Fox would like to sanitize her since she played a significant role in elevating McCarthy to the speakership. She must be a changed person or the GOP will have to ask itself some uncomfortable questions.

Things move fast, so cast your minds back only to 2021 when Mitch McConnell described Greene as a "cancer" on the Republican party and John Thune warned that the party had to draw some lines: "They have to decide who they want to be. Do they want to be the party of limited government and fiscal responsibility, free markets, peace through strength and pro life, or do they want to be the party of conspiracy theories and QAnon?"

On his Sunday show, Kurtz teed up opportunities for Greene to cleanse herself in the healing Fox font, inviting her to express her frustration with fellow members of the Freedom Caucus, and marveling that a Republican would decline to take a call Greene had placed to Donald Trump on her cellphone. Kurtz next advanced to the touchy topic of Greene's bat-guano views, but introduced it this way: "Just to deal with one bit of history, the Democrats stripped you of committee assignments—which was raw politics."

No, actually, it was civic hygiene. It was what the GOP would have done itself if it retained a shred of integrity.

Kurtz continued: "But in fairness, didn't you say around that time that you'd been a follower of QAnon conspiracy theory and you had rethought this and you were no longer influenced by the group?" Greene seized the opportunity to refashion herself:

"Like a lot of people today, I had easily gotten sucked into some things I had seen on the internet. But that was dealt with quickly early on. I never campaigned on those things. That was not something I believed in. That's not what I ran for Congress on. So those are so far in the past."

The bad internet sucked her in and forced her to believe that the Parkland shooting and the Sandy Hook murders and the Las Vegas massacre were all false flag operations; that 9/11 was an inside job; that a California wildfire was caused by Jewish space lasers; and that Hillary Clinton had murdered a child in order to use her blood for a satanic ritual.

"So far in the past." She hasn't said those things since 2018! Except, wait, wasn't it just in February 2022 that Greene spoke at a conference sponsored by the white nationalist/fascist Nick Fuentes? That was also the month that she described the Jan. 6 defendants as political prisoners and denounced "Nancy Pelosi's gazpacho police." (Though, candidly, we owe her a debt of gratitude for that.) And if memory serves, in October 2022, she told a crowd that "Democrats want Republicans dead and they have already started the killings." And wasn't it in December 2022—last month—that she told the New York Young Republican Club that if she and Steve Bannon had organized the Jan. 6 insurrection, "We would have won. Not to mention, it would have been armed."

Greene's makeover didn't start this week. She's made stabs at resets before, even traveling to the Holocaust museum to introduce a few facts into the roiling stew of garbage between her ears. She denounced Nick Fuentes after Trump dined with him (but not Trump), and acknowledged that a plane really did hit the Pentagon on 9/11. She has sparred with Lauren Boebert, the pillow guy and Alex Jones' fans. But this is not a case of a politician who misspeaks or commits a gaffe and must make amends. She has a disordered personality. As a grown adult, she chased a teenager who had survived the Parkland school shooting down the street, harassing and berating him. She is drawn to hatred as a moth to a flame. She is the poison that courses through the veins of parts of the right—the vicious, reality-challenged right. If she is to be normalized by the GOP, it is the party, not she, that is changed.

No sooner did McCarthy achieve election on Friday night than Greene rushed to his side. They posed for a grinning photo. It was his first act as speaker.

About the Author

Mona Charen is a syndicated columnist and political analyst. She received her undergraduate degree at Barnard College, Columbia University, with honors. Ms. Charen also holds a degree in law from George Washington University.

Ms. Charen began her career at National Review magazine, where she served as editorial assistant. On her first tax return at the age of 22, Ms. Charen listed her occupation as "pundit," explaining later, "You have to think big."

In 1984, Ms. Charen joined the White House staff, serving first as Nancy Reagan's speechwriter and later as associate director of the Office of Public Liaison. In the latter post, she lectured widely on the administration's Central America policy. Later in her White House career, she worked in the Public Affairs office, helping to craft the president's communications strategy.

In 1986, Ms. Charen left the White House to join the presidential campaign of then-Congressman Jack Kemp as a speechwriter.

Ms. Charen launched her syndicated column in 1987, and it has become one of the most widely read columns in the industry. It is featured in more than 150 newspapers and websites.

She spent six years as a regular commentator on CNN's "Capital Gang" and "Capital Gang Sunday," and has served as a judge of the Pulitzer Prizes. She has served as a fellow at the Hudson Institute and the Jewish Policy Center and is the author of three books: "Useful Idiots: How Liberals Got it Wrong in the Cold War and Still Blame America First" (2003); "Do-Gooders: How Liberals Harm Those They Claim to Help—and the Rest of Us" (2005); and "Sex Matters: How Modern Feminism Lost Touch with Science, Love, and Common Sense" (2018).

In 2010, she received the Eric Breindel Award for Excellence in Opinion Journalism.

Ms. Charen is now policy editor of The Bulwark and host of the "Beg to Differ" podcast. She lives in the Washington, D.C., area with her husband and three sons.

HARD RIGHT: THE GOP'S DRIFT TOWARD EXTREMISM
is also available as an e-book
for Kindle, Amazon Fire, iPad, Nook and
Android e-readers. Visit
creatorspublishing.com to learn more.

○ ○ ○

CREATORS PUBLISHING

We find compelling storytellers and
help them craft their narrative,
distributing their novels and collections
worldwide.

○ ○ ○

Made in United States
Orlando, FL
20 October 2023